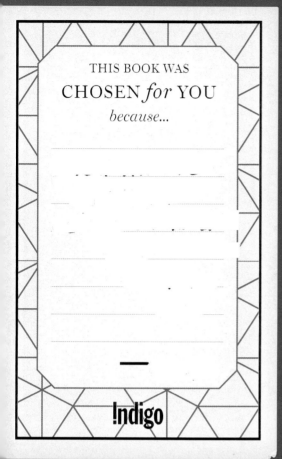

THIS BOOK WAS
CHOSEN *for* **YOU**
because...

!ndigo

Mary knows that home cooks, with so much going on in our lives, just want simple ingredients, straightforward techniques, and big flavors, and her new book, *In Mary's Kitchen*, is full of all three. And if those weren't enough, Mary also provides loads of bonus kitchen wisdom to help you get ahead, no matter what recipe you're making. With chapters organized by main ingredient, you'll find exactly what you need in next to no time.

Dive into *In Mary's Kitchen* with recipes for:

* **EGGS & THINGS** like Lemon Almond Blueberry Muffins and Green Eggs sans Ham

* **VEG & STARCH** like Romaine & Endive Salad with Anchovy Lemon Dressing & Crispy Breadcrumbs and Stewed White Beans with Greens & Chili

* **PASTA** like Pantry Puttanesca and Creamy Spaghetti al Limone

* **CHICKEN** like Sheet Pan Sunday Roast and Chick Parm Meatballs

* **BEEF, PORK & LAMB** like French Onion Pot Roast with Gruyère Potatoes and Brine & Bake Pork Chops

* And, of course, **SWEETS** like Raspberry Cheesecake Blondies and Almond Cherry Brownie Pudding

With every recipe Mary writes, her goal is to show you that cooking for yourself, your friends, and your family doesn't have to be boring, difficult, or stressful. No matter the time of day, or day of the week, *In Mary's Kitchen* is packed with uncomplicated, delicious recipes and loaded with tips and tricks to produce flavorful results—every time.

In Mary's Kitchen

STRESS-FREE RECIPES FOR EVERY HOME COOK

Mary Berg

appetite
by RANDOM HOUSE

Appetite by Random House® and colophon are registered trademarks of Penguin Random House LLC.

Library and Archives Canada Cataloguing in Publication is available upon request.

ISBN: 9780525611943
eBook ISBN: 9780525611950

Cover and book design by Jennifer Griffiths
Cover and book photography by Lauren Vandenbrook
Art direction by Jenna Mariash
Printed in China

Published in Canada by Appetite by Random House®,
a division of Penguin Random House LLC.
www.penguinrandomhouse.ca

10 9 8 7 6 5 4 3 2

appetite | Penguin
by RANDOM HOUSE | Random House
Canada

For Lindsay,
the loudest cheerleader
I could ever hope for.

Contents

1 *Introduction*
3 *Stress-Free Sidekick*
7 *Ingredients for Success*

Eggs & Things

12 Chipotle Breakfast Burritos
15 Herbed Blinis a.k.a. Savory Pancakes
16 Freeze & Fry Breakfast Sausage
19 Crispy Mini Rösti
20 Green Eggs sans Ham
23 Red Pepper Hummus Tartines
24 Lemon Almond Blueberry Muffins
27 Chocolate Hazelnut Croissant French Toast Bake
28 Soft Fruit Freezer Compote
31 Apple Cinnamon Biscuit Buns
33 Oat Crepes with Sweet Mascarpone & Blackberries

Veg & Starch

38 Pan con Tomate
41 Irish Onion Soup
42 Green Ginger Miso Soup
45 Lemony Lentil Soup
46 Buffalo Roasted Cauliflower & Chickpea Pitas with Blue Cheese Slaw
48 Black Bean Chipotle Veggie Burger
51 Crispy Garlic Parmesan Potatoes with Roasted Garlic Mayo
52 Spicy Roasted Sweet Potatoes
55 Green Couscous Salad
56 Fried Feta Salad with Honey & Herbs
59 Romaine & Endive Salad with Anchovy Lemon Dressing & Crispy Breadcrumbs
61 Bistro Salad
63 Eggplant Parmesan
66 Creamed Corn Baked Feta
69 Caramelized Shallots with Sherry Vinegar & Pistachios
70 Parmesan Zucchini with Crispy Chickpeas & Tahini Ricotta
73 Balsamic Grilled Radicchio & Pears
74 Smoky Harissa Eggplant with Herby Feta Oil & Pine Nuts
77 Roasted Mushrooms with Blue Cheese Rosemary Crumb
78 Green Veg Gratin
81 Pan-Fried Halloumi with Greens & Romesco
82 Curried Red Lentil–Stuffed Squash
84 Stewed White Beans with Greens & Chili
87 Quick Coconut Butter Tofu with Chickpeas
88 Creamy Polenta with Greens, Tomatoes & Cheese
91 Mushroom Stroganoff

Pasta

94 Creamy Spaghetti al Limone
97 Pantry Puttanesca
98 Caprese Baked Rigatoni alla Vodka
101 Miso Butter Corn Pasta
103 Mushroom & Pesto Skillet Lasagna
107 Creamy Lobster Gnocchi
109 Spicy Sausage Pasta with Rapini & Herbed Ricotta

Fish

114 Baked Fish Butty
117 Sesame Shrimpies
119 Crispy Coconut Fish Tacos
121 Smoked Fish Brandade

125 Lemony Shrimp with White Beans & Garlic Toast
126 Seared Carrot Ginger Salmon
129 Lemony Piccata
130 Tomato Trout
133 Mediterranean Salmon

Chicken

137 Satay Chicken Wings with Peanut Sauce
139 Chipotle Chicken Soup
143 Sheet Pan Souvlaki
145 Chick Parm Meatballs
149 Roasted Garlic Bread Chicken Thighs
150 BLT Chicken
153 Fresh & Grilled Ratatouille with Provençal Chicken
155 Chicken Noodle Roast Chicken
159 Sheet Pan Sunday Roast

Beef, Pork & Lamb

165 Pizza Today/Pizza Tomorrow
167 Creamy Harissa Lamb Meatballs
171 Roasted Sausage Sheet Pan Dinner
172 Brine & Bake Pork Chops
175 Cider Pork Tenderloin with Autumn Veg
177 French Onion Pot Roast with Gruyère Potatoes
179 Bacon-Wrapped Meatloaf
183 Reverse-Sear Steak with Chimichurri
185 Roast Beef Bourguignon

Sweets

190 My Dream Chocolate Chip Cookie
191 Ginger Molasses Cookies
195 Whatever You Like Slice & Bake Cookies
197 Raspberry Cheesecake Blondies
200 Marble Zucchini Loaf with Chocolate Cinnamon Streusel
203 Coconut Loaf with Chocolate Hazelnut Glaze
205 Lemon Cornmeal Olive Oil Cake
207 Tiramisu Cupcakes
211 Chocolate Peanut Butter Cake with Cornflake Crunch
213 Basic Pastry
219 Fresh Strawberry Pie with Stable Whipped Cream
221 Cinnamon Cream Cheese & Peach Galette
223 Mary's Lemon Meringue Pie
225 Black Forest Tart
228 Blackberry Apple Cream Cheese Cobbler
231 Cannoli Bougatsa
233 Dulce de Leche Pavlova
235 Spiced Apple Cheesecake
239 Grilled Stone-Fruit Melba
240 Almond Cherry Brownie Pudding

Basics

244 Chicken Stock
245 Vegetable Broth
246 My Go-To Pesto
247 No-Yeast Flatbread
248 Basic Polenta

251 *Thank You!*
253 *Index*

Introduction

At the risk of being obvious, the kitchen is truly my favorite place in the world. It's the one place where my relatively busy mind calms, where the stresses of life melt away, and time seems to slow down. As I slice shallots, stir a pot of simmering sauce, knead dough into a soft and stretchy pillow, or watch bubbling butter begin to brown, everything that felt so big before I started cooking just seems to become more manageable.

When I first made the switch from office work to cooking and recipe writing full time, I was nervous that I might lose that spark. Cooking had always been my hobby, that comforting thing I could confidently do no matter how I was feeling on any given day. Luckily, that never went away. Food continues to be my passion.

But according to the scuttlebutt on the street, not everyone feels this (admittedly over-the-top) poetic love for their daily trips to the stove. Apparently, some people even *loathe* their kitchens with the fieriness of a thousand flambés!

Can you believe it?!

Maybe you can! Maybe you're even one of those people. Or perhaps you just find the daily trudge of making food humdrum at best. No matter what end of that spectrum you find yourself on, I am here to help.

With pretty much every single recipe I write, my goal is to show you that cooking for yourself, your friends, and your family doesn't have to be boring, difficult, or stressful. But with my new book, I'm aiming to make your life even easier, with uncomplicated but delicious recipes packed with tips and tricks that you can carry with you into everything you cook.

As with all my recipes, the food in these pages is made using ingredients that can be easily found at an average grocery store or even in your own pantry. If a specialty ingredient is called for, I'll either tell you where you can find it and how else to use it, so any leftovers don't sit forgotten in the back of your fridge, or I'll provide tips on how to substitute something else. I've used basic kitchen equipment throughout because there is nothing more disheartening to beginners and seasoned cooks alike than finding a recipe that piques your interest only to realize you don't have the tools to make it.

As always, cooking and sharing food should be as much about comfort and enjoyment as they are about sustenance and nourishment. Filled with ideas that will take you from breakfast through to dessert in chapters broken down according to their main ingredient to facilitate easy searching, *In Mary's Kitchen* is here to share with you the simple pleasure of straightforward, cookable recipes that will hopefully make the kitchen your happy place too.

Mary xo

Stress-Free Sidekick

People often tell me that the thing they like best about my recipes is that I make it all look so easy. But being neither an actor nor a very good liar, I feel like I've been given too much credit. It all looks so easy because it *is* easy! While I've been known to tackle difficult and intricate recipes in the past, over the past few years, all I really want to do is make good food as simply as possible. Life is stressful enough—cooking shouldn't have to be.

Now, a lot of people assume that simple and straightforward cooking requires five ingredients or fewer, a quick method, or little to no effort, but I don't think that those things alone make for an easy time in the kitchen and delicious results. Consider the five-ingredient rule: if a dish only contains a handful of ingredients, each one has to do *a lot* of heavy lifting. If you mess up on any one element, there's no room to hide. And while some fast or no-effort recipes work beautifully, those things alone do not guarantee a stress-free time getting a delicious dinner on the table.

When working on any recipe I'm going to put out into the world for you lovely people to make, I have a hard and fast rule: a recipe needs to taste better than the effort put in would suggest. I call this my 30:70 rule—a recipe should at most require 30 percent effort leaving you with a delicious 70 percent payoff. For instance, the amount of work that goes into, let's say, a homemade New York–style cheesecake is not insubstantial, but, with a little help and know-how, the payoff is totally worth it. Now, the effort that goes into homemade croissants? Too much, in my opinion. I'd rather leave that to the professionals and take a stroll to my favorite local bakery for a fresh and flaky treat.

To be your stress-free sidekick in the kitchen and provide you with recipes that are doable for beginners while still being snazzy enough for seasoned home cooks, I try to put myself in someone else's shoes and find the things that I do without even thinking. My rough drafts of recipes look like haunted pirate maps that even I can hardly decipher. But when I sit down to actually type them out, I try to flesh out tips that I've learned while spending pretty much every waking minute thinking about food, from prep and cooking, to serving and cleanup, that make cooking easy and natural to me. I call these the "whys" of a recipe. Having always been an inquisitive person, finding out why a recipe asks me to do or add something is the key to me remembering it, and allowing it to become part of my kitchen routine. While I've always tried to weave these culinary fun facts into recipe methods, in this book, I wanted to highlight recipe "whys." In each recipe, you'll find a note containing a tip or trick that not only applies to that recipe but can act as a building block for all your culinary endeavors.

With these recipes, I don't just want to help you be a good cook within the pages of this book. My hope is that they will help teach and convince you that you are the amazing, talented, stress-free cook I know you are. I want to show you that you *can* make your own pizza dough, your own chicken stock, your own pesto, your own whatever, but also that you don't have to in order to be successful in the kitchen! I don't want you to think of taking a shortcut or picking something up at the grocery store to help you get food on the table as "cheating." If you ever feel this way, think of my cousin Lindsay who once wisely said to someone at a baby shower who asked if she had baked the cookies she brought: "I made the money that bought them . . . so, yes."

Within this book and in the kitchen in general, there is no such thing as cheating, just as there is no such thing as failure. Nothing should make you feel down, defeated, or bad, whether you nail a recipe the first time or the seventh, or take every grocery store shortcut you can think of. Everything about food, from the recipes in this book and beyond, should make you feel happy, full, and comforted (other than the dirty dishes, of course).

No matter what, feeding yourself, your friends, and your family is a small victory you get to be proud of every single day. I'm so excited for you to make these recipes your own, and I can't wait to join you for the ride.

Ingredients for Success

A well-stocked kitchen is a stress-free kitchen. Here is a quick rundown of the things I keep in my cupboards and fridge as well as a few tips and tricks I've picked up along the way that help keep me culinarily carefree.

SALT, SEASONING & SPICES

My go-to **salt** for both cooking and baking is kosher. Diamond Crystal kosher salt is my brand of choice and what you can find gracing my salt pig, but if you prefer to use sea salt in your kitchen, I suggest using slightly less than what is called for in the recipes as sea salt is brinier than kosher, giving whatever you add it to a saltier flavor.

Black pepper is always freshly ground but most other **spices** in my cupboard, with the exception of coriander seeds and nutmeg, are pre-ground. I suggest buying smaller amounts more frequently from spice or bulk food stores as they are not only more affordable, but they will also keep your spice cupboard tidier and less likely to be the site of a spice-based archaeological dig.

FATS

During the COVID-19 pandemic as I tried to find bright spots in the everyday, I began treating myself to fancy **butter**. I don't think I'll ever go back, but if the price tag gives you sticker shock, commercial butter will work perfectly in every recipe in this book. In most ingredient lists, I simply indicate "butter," and in those instances, use whatever you have on hand. However, in a few particular recipes where unsalted butter is specified, it's worth making sure you use it.

For **oils**, my pantry staples are canola oil (though any neutral-flavored oil makes a great substitute), an extra virgin olive oil for cooking that won't break the bank, and a super peppery finishing extra virgin olive oil for those dishes where the oil is not heated. Within the recipes in this book, the more budget-friendly cooking olive oil is referred to as "olive oil" while the fancy stuff is "extra virgin olive oil." While your cooking olive oil will work in both instances, save pricey bottles for no-heat applications.

For ease of use, I like to transfer my canola oil and cooking olive oil into squeeze bottles, though if you are strict with measurements, they can make your pours a little heavy-handed.

MEATS & FISH

Most recipes for **poultry**, **beef**, **pork**, and **lamb** call for the meat to be removed from the fridge to "come up to room temperature" before cooking. While the

temperature won't technically rise that much, it will take the chill of the fridge off and help the internal temperature come up more quickly and easily when cooking, giving you better results.

PRODUCE

Dark leafy greens such as kale, spinach, Swiss chard, or collards are all interchangeable in this book. Just keep whatever you like best on hand and wilt or cook until tender, being aware that spinach and chard will cook faster than heartier greens like kale and collards.

Herbs can be placed into two categories: woody and fine. Herbs like rosemary, thyme, sage, and oregano are all considered woody, while herbs like basil, parsley, chives, and tarragon are fine. I find they are all pretty interchangeable according to your taste, as long as you stick to those categories. The only real outlier in the world of herbs is cilantro. If you or someone you're cooking for hates the taste, I suggest substituting Italian or Thai basil. If you are going from fresh to dried, the general conversion rate is three to one.

As I hate mincing **garlic** (so finicky and garlicky-cutting-boardy!), I always reach for my rasp and finely grate the cloves straight into a dish. If you're a garlic press fan or don't mind finely chopping garlic, feel free to mince that way.

DAIRY & EGGS

All **dairy** is full fat, including cheese, cream cheese, sour cream, and yogurt. For milk, I use whole, though 2 percent can be used if that is what you keep in your fridge. When a recipe calls for cream, the type or fat percentage will be specified and should not be substituted unless otherwise stated. The specific fat percentage of cream helps keep it from curdling when heated or mixed with acidic ingredients.

All recipes use large **eggs** and, when using in baking, try to bring them up to room temperature by leaving them on the counter for 30 minutes or by placing them in a bowl of warm water for a few minutes. This will help the eggs emulsify into the mixture and keep them from rechilling room-temperature butter, which could lead to a curdled batter.

TOOLS FOR SUCCESS

Despite my general style falling somewhere in the maximalist sphere, when it comes to my **kitchen equipment**, I'm a minimalist. There is nothing that stresses me out more than kitchen clutter, so while I understand the allure of gadgets like spiralizers, bread machines, and electric pressure cookers, my recipes require minimal equipment and tools. Here is a bare-bones list of what I use in my kitchen to keep things simple, straightforward, and stress-free:

* Eight-inch chef's knife
* One large wooden and one large plastic cutting board (your cutting boards should be large enough that your longest knife can lie diagonally across it with at least an inch of extra room on both ends)
* Fine rasp or Microplane
* Heat-resistant spatula
* Wooden spoons
* Metal whisks
* Glass, metal, or ceramic mixing bowls
* Hand mixer or stand mixer
* An eight- to twelve-cup food processor with grating and slicing attachments
* Immersion blender, smoothie blender, or stand blender
* Fine-mesh sieve
* Ten-inch cast-iron skillet
* Five-quart Dutch oven
* Large and small saucepan, with lids
* Stainless sauté pan and skillet
* Nonstick skillet
* A few half-sheet pans
* A standard set of baking pans
* Parchment paper and heavy-duty aluminum foil
* Nine-inch springform pan, ten-inch removable-bottom tart pan, and a Bundt pan, if you like baking

Eggs & Things

Chipotle Breakfast Burritos

MAKES 8 BURRITOS

12 eggs

¼ cup milk

2 tablespoons pureed or finely chopped chipotle peppers in adobo sauce (see note)

Kosher salt

Freshly ground black pepper

4 green onions, thinly sliced

2 handfuls spinach, roughly chopped

¾ cup cherry tomatoes, halved, optional

8 medium or large flour tortillas

1½–2 cups canned refried beans

2 cups shredded cheese, preferably Tex-Mex

Note:

Whenever I'm using chipotle peppers in adobo sauce in a recipe, I like to blitz the whole can into a puree and store any leftovers in a container or zip-top bag in the freezer. The puree is easy to scoop even when frozen, and freezing any leftovers allows the can to last for months.

This recipe is inspired by my best friend, Marisa, the ultimate breakfast maker. Any time I visit her, I know I'm starting my days with a hearty meal that usually includes a breakfast burrito stuffed with eggs, cheese, and whatever veg she has in the fridge. With these chipotle breakfast burritos, I've taken as many shortcuts as I can and batched them up to stash in my freezer for those days when I only have time to grab something as I run out the door.

Preheat your oven to 425°F and lightly grease a 9-by-13-inch baking pan with nonstick cooking spray.

In a large bowl, beat the eggs, milk, and chipotles together and season with salt and pepper. Stir in the green onions, spinach, and tomatoes and transfer to the prepared baking pan. Bake the eggs for 15 minutes, until set. Set aside to cool slightly, and then cut the baked eggs into eight equal pieces.

Lay out the tortillas and spread the refried beans down the center of each.

Heat a large skillet over medium-high heat.

Place a slice of the baked eggs on top of the refried beans and scatter with cheese. If using smaller tortillas, simply fold over both sides to create an open-ended roll. If using large tortillas, tuck in the top and bottom and roll up for a more classic sealed burrito.

Working in batches, place the burritos in the pan, seam side down, and cook until golden and crisp, about 2 minutes. Flip and cook on the other side for another 2 minutes until crisp.

At this point, you can serve the burritos or set aside to cool completely to room temperature.

Wrap the cooled burritos in a square of parchment paper then place in a freezer bag. Store in the freezer for up to 2 months.

To reheat the burritos, defrost overnight in the fridge, unwrap, and heat in a toaster oven or a skillet set over medium heat for 3 to 4 minutes per side. If reheating from frozen, heat in the microwave for 3 to 5 minutes on the defrost setting. You can then heat in the microwave for 1 to 2 minutes or until hot or unwrap and heat as directed above.

Herbed Blinis a.k.a. Savory Pancakes

SERVES 3 TO 4

FAST FLAVOR

GET AHEAD

1¼ cups all-purpose flour

1 teaspoon sugar

1 teaspoon baking powder

½ teaspoon baking soda

½ teaspoon kosher salt

¼ teaspoon freshly ground black pepper

1½ cups buttermilk

1 egg, separated

3 tablespoons finely chopped herbs, such as chives, parsley, dill, or tarragon + extra for serving

4 tablespoons butter, divided

2–3 teaspoons olive oil, divided

½ cup sour cream

5 oz cold- or hot-smoked salmon

½ lemon, cut into wedges

Note:

For a slightly nuttier flavor, swap ½ cup of the all-purpose flour with ½ cup of spelt, buckwheat, or whole wheat flour. As whole-grain flour absorbs more liquid than all-purpose, you will need to add another 2 to 4 tablespoons of milk to reach a pancake batter consistency.

While I would never turn down a classic pancake breakfast, a sweet stack tends to leave me hungry an hour after eating. As a savory breakfast gal, these herbed pancakes are a quick and perfect starchy base for breakfast classics like smoked salmon or bacon and eggs when I've run out of toast.

Place a large nonstick skillet over medium heat and turn your oven on to 200°F.

In a large bowl, whisk together the flour, sugar, baking powder, baking soda, salt, and pepper.

In a separate bowl or large glass measuring cup, whisk together the buttermilk, egg yolk, and herbs. Add 2 tablespoons of butter into the pan to melt. Once melted, stir into the buttermilk mixture.

In a small bowl, whip the egg white until it is foamy and soft peaks hold, about 30 seconds.

Add the buttermilk mixture to the dry ingredients and mix just until almost combined. Add the egg white and gently fold in. You do not want the mixture to be completely smooth, so err on the side of less mixing.

Add 1 tablespoon of butter to the pan along with 1 teaspoon of oil. Spoon about ¼ cup of batter per pancake into the pan and cook until golden and crisp around the edges, 2 to 3 minutes per side. Transfer the pancakes onto a baking rack set over a sheet pan and keep warm in the oven while you cook the remaining batter. Add more butter and oil to the pan as needed.

To serve, top with sour cream and smoked salmon as well as a scattering of fresh herbs, with a lemon wedge on the side.

As with any homemade pancakes, these can be made in advance. Separate each pancake with a small square of parchment or wax paper and transfer to a zip-top freezer bag. Freeze for up to 2 months. To reheat, separate the pancakes, remove the parchment paper, and cook in a toaster or toaster oven until hot and crisp.

BANG FOR
YOUR BUCK

FAST
FLAVOR

GET
AHEAD

Freeze & Fry Breakfast Sausage

MAKES 8 PATTIES

1 lb ground pork

3 tablespoons maple syrup

2 garlic cloves, finely grated

1 teaspoon ground sage

1 teaspoon dried thyme

1 teaspoon fennel seeds, crushed

¼ teaspoon smoked paprika

1 teaspoon kosher salt

¼–½ teaspoon freshly ground black pepper

Olive oil, for cooking

As a kid, I wasn't a picky eater per se, but I did have a couple of things that would knock it out of the park every single time. Cheese tortellini with butter and shaky cheese (the stuff that comes in the can), white rice with a can of tuna and some soy sauce mixed in, Italian chili (a.k.a. just a bowl of meat sauce), and pancakes and "chachiches," garbled three-year-old speak for breakfast sausages, were always hits in our house. By making freezer-friendly sausage patties from scratch, you can tailor them to your and your family's tastes. This is my family's favorite combo. Sweet, smoky, herby, and a little peppery—great as a side to eggs and toast or on a breakfast sandwich, or take a cue from a young Mary Berg and serve them alongside pancakes doused in maple syrup.

Note:

Like with any ground meat patties, as they cook, the protein contracts, making them shrink in diameter and puff up in the middle. This is why some burger recipes call for a thumbprint to be pressed in the center of each patty before cooking. By pressing these into thin ¼-inch-thick sausage patties, you will end up with perfect breakfast sausages as opposed to weird breakfast meatballs.

Add the pork, maple syrup, garlic, sage, thyme, fennel seeds, paprika, salt, and pepper to a large bowl and, using two forks or your fingers, gently mix until well combined.

Using a spring-loaded ice cream scoop or a large tablespoon, divide the mixture into twelve equal balls and press into ¼-inch-thick patties.

If cooking immediately, heat 1 to 2 teaspoons of oil in a large skillet set over medium-high heat. Working in batches, cook the sausage until browned on both sides and the meat is cooked through, about 2 minutes per side.

If freezing, transfer the patties to a parchment-lined sheet pan, cover, and place in the freezer until solid. Transfer the frozen patties to a freezer bag and store in the freezer for up to 3 months.

To cook from frozen, heat 1 to 2 teaspoons of oil in a large skillet set over medium heat. Cook the frozen patties on each side for 2 to 3 minutes until golden, then continue to cook, flipping frequently, until cooked through to 160°F.

Crispy Mini Rösti

SERVES 4 TO 6

2–3 large (1 lb) russet potatoes

2 medium (10½ oz) sweet potatoes

1½ teaspoons kosher salt

½ small red or yellow onion, thinly sliced

Freshly ground black pepper

½ teaspoon garlic powder

2 tablespoons melted butter

2 tablespoons olive oil

3 oz extra-old cheddar, grated

½ cup sour cream or plain Greek yogurt

Thinly sliced chives or green onion tops, for garnish

Note:

Wringing the potatoes might seem like an unnecessary step, but excess moisture is the enemy of golden-brown crispiness. This rule is true for pretty much everything you cook.

The quest toward crispy potatoes doesn't begin and end with the perfect side to a Sunday roast. Breakfast potatoes deserve a bit of that crispy action too. By shrinking them down to the size of classic stove-top rösti and roasting them in a hot oven, I've maximized the surface area, resulting in crispy golden-brown potato nests with tender and fluffy insides. The final addition of some cheese sprinkled on top helps hold everything together and makes these even more delish when served as part of a classic breakfast spread.

Preheat your oven to 450°F and spray a 12-cup muffin tin with nonstick cooking spray.

Gently scrub the potatoes and sweet potatoes and grate on the large side of a box grater. By keeping the skins on, you're reducing food waste and increasing your fiber intake. Transfer to a mesh strainer set in the sink and season with the salt. Set aside for 5 to 10 minutes to draw out some of the water.

Using your hands or a clean kitchen towel, wring out as much water as possible from the potatoes and transfer to a large bowl. Add the onion, season with salt, pepper, and the garlic powder, then pour the butter and oil overtop. Stir well to combine.

Divide the potato mixture into the wells of the muffin tin and press down firmly with a tablespoon. Roast for 25 to 30 minutes or until golden on top and the edges are crisp.

Scatter the top with the cheddar cheese and place under a high broiler for 1 to 2 minutes or until the cheese is melted and lightly golden.

Serve topped with a dollop of sour cream and a scattering of chives.

Green Eggs sans Ham

SERVES 2

1 teaspoon olive oil

1 garlic clove, finely grated

Kosher salt

Freshly ground black pepper

2–3 large handfuls spinach

2–3 tablespoons basil pesto

4 eggs

Toasted sourdough,
   for serving

Note:

Store-bought pesto works
well, but pesto is a cinch
to make. Find my favorite
recipe on page 246.

These green eggs are a super quick breakfast perfect for weekday mornings when I've only got a few spare minutes, but they also look fancy enough to wow overnight guests. Being a non ham eater, I stick to the recipe below, but if you'd like to transform these into something that someone named Sam might like, dice and crisp up two strips of bacon or four thin slices of pancetta in the pan and use the rendered fat in place of the oil.

Place a large cast-iron or nonstick skillet over medium heat. Add the oil and garlic, season with salt and pepper, and cook for 30 seconds. Toss in the spinach, season with more salt and pepper, and allow it to wilt for about 30 seconds.

Stir in the basil pesto and divide the mixture into two low piles in the pan. Crack and divide the eggs over the spinach mixture and fry until the whites are set and the yolks are still runny, 2 to 3 minutes.

Season the eggs with salt and pepper and serve immediately beside or on top of toasted sourdough.

Note: Beans straight from the can, though perfect for salads, soups, and adding to a variety of other dishes, are a little too firm to blitz into a creamy dip. By simmering the chickpeas with a bit of baking soda until very soft, the end result will be perfectly smooth and velvety hummus.

Red Pepper Hummus Tartines

SERVES 2 WITH LEFTOVER HUMMUS

FAST
FLAVOR

GET
AHEAD

ONE
POT-ISH

¼ small red onion, thinly sliced

2 tablespoons red wine vinegar

Kosher salt

3 teaspoons olive oil

2 eggs

2 slices sourdough or whole-
grain bread

1 garlic clove, halved

4–6 tablespoons hummus,
recipe follows

¼ cup chopped roasted
red peppers

1–2 oz crumbled feta cheese

Coarsely chopped fine
herbs, such as basil, chives,
oregano, or parsley

Freshly ground black pepper

Hummus is one of my favorite breakfast add-ons. It's creamy, flavorful, full of protein, and goes with pretty much any savory thing you want to put on top of it. This is my go-to topping combination, but feel free to follow wherever your breakfast cravings take you.

In a small bowl, stir together the onion and vinegar, and season with salt. Set aside to lightly pickle.

Heat the oil in a nonstick skillet over medium-high heat. Add the eggs and fry until the whites are set and crisp around the edges but the yolk is still runny, 2 to 3 minutes.

Toast the sourdough, and then rub the cut side of garlic onto the hot toast. Spread the hummus overtop and scatter with the roasted red peppers. Place a fried egg on top and scatter with feta and herbs. Using a fork, scoop some of the onions from the vinegar and sprinkle overtop. Season with salt and pepper, and serve.

Hummus

1 can (19 fl oz) chickpeas

½ teaspoon baking soda

Kosher salt

1–2 lemons, juiced

¼ cup tahini

2 garlic cloves, finely grated

½ teaspoon cumin

¼ cup extra virgin olive oil

Drain and rinse the chickpeas and add to a small saucepan along with the baking soda. Cover with a couple inches of cold water, season with ½ teaspoon of salt, and simmer for 20 minutes or until the chickpeas are very soft and can be easily mashed when pinched between your fingers.

Strain and rinse the chickpeas and transfer to a food processor or high-speed blender. Add the juice of one lemon along with the tahini, garlic, and cumin. Process until smooth, then, with the mixer running, slowly stream in the oil. If the mixture is a little thick, add a couple tablespoons of cold water, blitzing after each addition, until the mixture has reached your desired consistency. Season to taste with salt and more lemon, if needed.

Transfer the hummus to a container and store in the fridge for up to 1 week.

Lemon Almond Blueberry Muffins

MAKES 6 LARGE MUFFINS

3 tablespoons melted butter

½ cup sugar

1 egg

½ cup sour cream or plain yogurt

½ lemon, zested

½ teaspoon vanilla extract

½ teaspoon almond extract

1 cup + 2 teaspoons all-purpose flour, divided

½ teaspoon ground cardamom

½ teaspoon baking powder

¼ teaspoon baking soda

¼ teaspoon kosher salt

¾ cup fresh or frozen blueberries

FOR THE STREUSEL TOPPING

¼ cup packed brown sugar

3 tablespoons all-purpose flour

¼ cup sliced almonds

¼ teaspoon kosher salt

¼ teaspoon ground cardamom

2 tablespoons melted butter

Note:

Muffins benefit from as little mixing as possible. Their texture is also improved by a rest before baking. This allows the flour to hydrate, lets any gluten that has been worked up relax, and gives the baking powder time to activate, giving your muffins more lift and a finer texture.

Perhaps it's a hazard of the job, but sometimes I find myself with too many baked goods hanging around. If I know that I'm not having anyone pop by for a few days or have no plans to venture out into the world, a dozen muffins can quickly turn into a bit of a chore to get through. In my house, half a dozen muffins is the perfect amount for a normal week, but if you're a big family or want to bring something into the office, this recipe is easily doubled.

Preheat your oven to 375°F and line six wells of a muffin tin with paper liners.

In a large bowl, whisk together the butter, sugar, egg, sour cream, lemon zest, vanilla extract, and almond extract until well combined. In a separate bowl, whisk 1 cup of the flour with the cardamom, baking powder, baking soda, and salt. Add the dry ingredients to the wet and mix just until almost combined.

In a bowl, stir the blueberries with the remaining 2 teaspoons of flour to coat, then add to the muffin batter and gently mix just until evenly distributed.

If you have time, cover the bowl and set aside at room temperature for 1 hour or transfer to the fridge up to overnight.

Make the streusel by stirring together the brown sugar, flour, almonds, salt, and cardamom in a small bowl. Using your fingers, mix in the butter to make a clumpy streusel mixture.

Using two large spoons or a spring-loaded ice cream scoop, divide the batter between the paper liners and scatter each with some streusel.

Bake for 20 to 23 minutes or until golden brown and springy or a toothpick inserted into the center comes out clean.

Allow to cool slightly before serving. Store cooled muffins in a resealable bag or an airtight container for up to 3 days.

Chocolate Hazelnut Croissant French Toast Bake

SERVES 6

FOOD WASTE

GET AHEAD

SIMPLY SNAZZY

6 croissants, preferably day-old

¾ cup chocolate hazelnut spread

4 eggs

¾ cup milk

¼ cup cream

1 teaspoon vanilla extract

¼ cup sugar

4 teaspoons cocoa powder

¼ teaspoon cinnamon

¼ cup semi-sweet chocolate chips

Icing sugar, optional

Fresh berries

Overnight French toast is my go-to company-worthy breakfast that can be thrown together a few minutes before bed and stashed in the fridge, leaving you with nothing to do in the morning other than heating your oven, enjoying your coffee, and looking like you have it all together. I've given recipes for many overnight French toasts over the years, but this one is my new favorite.

Preheat your oven to 375°F and lightly grease a 9-inch round or square casserole dish. Split the croissants in half and spread each half with chocolate hazelnut spread. Arrange in the prepared baking dish, chocolate side up, so that they are slightly overlapping and set aside.

In a large mixing bowl, whisk the eggs and slowly add the milk, cream, and vanilla. Whisk in the sugar, cocoa powder, and cinnamon. Pour the custard mixture over the croissants and scatter with the chocolate chips. Gently press and smoosh the croissants down to ensure that they absorb the custard.

Allow the pan to sit at room temperature for 10 to 15 minutes or, if getting ahead, cover and refrigerate overnight.

Bake for 30 to 35 minutes or until golden, crisp, and set in the middle.

To serve, dust with icing sugar, if desired, and top with berries.

Note:

As with any custardy bread dishes such as French toast, bread pudding, or even your Thanksgiving stuffing, stale bread is the way to go. In this recipe, day-old croissants perfectly absorb all the custard without disintegrating.

Soft Fruit Freezer Compote

MAKES ABOUT 3 CUPS

1 cup sugar

4 cups chopped soft fruit,
such as berries or stone fruits

1 lemon or orange, zested
and juiced

1 sprig woody herbs, optional

½ teaspoon extract, such as
vanilla or almond, optional

MY FAVE FLAVOR COMBOS:

* Cherry sage vanilla
* Blackberry rosemary
almond
* Strawberry thyme vanilla
* Peach coconut
* Blueberry lavender

Note:

With less sugar than jam
and no added pectin, this is
not a shelf-stable preserve
and needs to be kept in the
freezer for long-term storage.

Like many people, I tend to get a little overzealous at the
grocery store or farmers' market during the spring and summer
months when fresh fruits are so plentiful. Back at home, when
the fruits start to turn a little sad, I grab a pot and some sugar
and whip up a batch of this compote. It's the perfect thing to
have on hand in your freezer for serving on toast, spreading
onto cookies and cakes, spooning over waffles, pancakes, or
yogurt, or even adding to a cheese board. Below I've given you
the basic proportions, and I've shared some of my fave flavor
combos as well, but feel free to experiment to suit your taste.

Add the sugar and half of the fruit into a large pot and, using a
wooden spoon or potato masher, mash together until the fruit is
broken down and combined with the sugar. Stir in the remaining
fruit, citrus juice, and herbs. For a more intense flavor from the
citrus fruit, you can also add the zest.

Place the pot over medium heat and bring the mixture to a boil,
stirring frequently. Turn the heat down to medium-low and simmer
for 10 to 20 minutes, or until thick and jammy. To test if your fruit is
thick enough to set, place a small plate in the freezer until very cold.
Spoon a little of the hot compote onto the cold plate and leave for
10 seconds. Give it a poke, and if it's somewhat jelly-like, it's done.

Remove the compote from the heat, fish out the herbs, if needed,
and stir in the extract. Allow the jam to cool completely.

Using straight-sided jars, plastic containers, or even small freezer
bags, divide the compote into 1-cup portions. Transfer to the fridge
to cool completely before moving any compote to the freezer. I like
to keep one portion in a jar or container in the fridge for use within
2 weeks and transfer the rest to the freezer for up to 3 months. If
using jars or containers for freezer storage, leave at least 2 inches of
head room at the top to allow for expansion, and check the jars or
containers for any cracks before defrosting and enjoying. If using
freezer bags, lay them flat until fully frozen to make storage easier
and defrosting faster.

Apple Cinnamon Biscuit Buns

MAKES 9 BISCUITS

FAST FLAVOR

GET AHEAD

FOR THE FILLING

4 tablespoons butter, divided

2 cups (about 2 large) apples, peeled and cut into ½-inch dice

½ cup packed brown sugar, divided

1 tablespoon cinnamon

¼ teaspoon kosher salt

½ cup chopped pecans

FOR THE BISCUIT DOUGH

2 cups all-purpose flour

1 tablespoon sugar

4 teaspoons baking powder

½ teaspoon baking soda

½ teaspoon kosher salt

5 tablespoons cold butter, cut into pats

1¼ cups cold buttermilk

1 teaspoon vanilla extract

FOR THE CREAM CHEESE FROSTING

½ cup brick-style cream cheese, room temperature

¼ cup icing sugar

½ teaspoon vanilla extract

¼ teaspoon cinnamon

There are a few things that I crave that require immediate attention and cinnamon buns are at the top of that list. Too bad they take a good few hours to make . . . until now! By combining fluffy and flaky biscuit dough with an apple pecan cinnamon filling, these babies satisfy that need for swirly cinnamon flavor in a flash.

For the filling, melt the butter over medium heat in a medium skillet. Scoop 2 tablespoons of the butter into a small dish and set aside for later. Add the apples and 2 tablespoons of the brown sugar into the skillet and cook, stirring occasionally, until softened and lightly caramelized, 8 to 10 minutes. Set aside to cool completely.

Meanwhile, in a small bowl, whisk the remaining 6 tablespoons of brown sugar with the cinnamon, salt, and pecans and set aside.

When the apples are cool, heat the oven to 450°F and lightly grease a 9-inch square baking pan with nonstick cooking spray.

For the biscuit dough, combine the flour, sugar, baking powder, baking soda, and salt in a large bowl. Toss in the cold butter and, using the tips of your fingers, pinch and snap it into the flour mixture until the pieces are about the size of a pea. In a glass measuring cup, combine the buttermilk and vanilla. Make a well in the center of the dry ingredients and add the buttermilk mixture. Stir just to combine, until a shaggy dough forms.

Turn the dough out onto a well-floured work surface. Press the dough down with your hands until it is about 1 inch thick, then fold it over onto itself like a book. Repeat this process two more times, then press the dough out into a 9-by-12-inch rectangle.

Spread the reserved melted butter over the dough and evenly sprinkle on the cinnamon-sugar-pecan mixture. Transfer the cooled apples onto the dough and spread them into an even layer. Starting at the long edge, roll the dough up into a swirled log, then cut into nine equal pieces. Arrange the buns in the prepared pan, cut side up. At this point, you can cover the pan and store in the fridge for up to 8 hours.

continued

Bake for 15 to 18 minutes or until golden brown and the center bun springs back when gently pressed.

While baking, make the cream cheese frosting by beating the cream cheese, icing sugar, vanilla, and cinnamon together until smooth.

Allow the buns to cool slightly or completely to room temperature before frosting. Store leftover buns in an airtight container for up to 2 days.

Note:

In most biscuit recipes, buttermilk measurements are often listed with a range in order to get the right texture and achieve light and flaky biscuits. For instance, on hot and humid days, the lower range called for will most likely do, while on drier days, your dough may need more buttermilk. With this recipe, however, a slightly stiffer dough is preferable as it is easier to fill and roll, so additional buttermilk is not needed.

Oat Crepes with Sweet Mascarpone & Blackberries

SERVES 4 TO 6

FOR THE CREPES

½ cup rolled oats

1¼ cups all-purpose flour

3 tablespoons sugar

¼ teaspoon kosher salt

1 cup milk

2 eggs

2 tablespoons melted butter

1 teaspoon vanilla extract

FOR THE TOPPING

1 cup mascarpone cheese

½ orange, zested and juiced

6 tablespoons packed brown sugar, divided

½ teaspoon cinnamon, divided

1½ teaspoons vanilla extract, divided

1 tablespoon butter

1 pint fresh blackberries

When I was about twelve years old, while my contemporaries were dipping their toes into the world of preteen dances and hand-holding, I was going through that classic phase all kids go through: my crepe phase. Savory, sweet, breakfast through dessert, crepes were always on the menu at the Berg house. Unlike butterfly clips and layering really long tank tops under too-tight polo shirts, I never grew out of that phase and have continued looking for ways to improve on the classic ever since. With a handful of oats and a swipe of sweetened mascarpone cheese, twenty years later, crepes are still my jam.

For the crepes, add the oats to a blender and blitz into a fine powder. Add the flour, sugar, and salt, and blitz to combine.

Pour in the milk along with ½ cup of water and add the eggs, butter, and vanilla. Blitz for 10 to 15 seconds or until the batter is smooth. Cover and transfer to the fridge for at least 30 minutes or up to overnight. This will allow the oats and flour to hydrate, giving the crepes a better texture and making them easier to cook.

When the batter has rested, heat a large nonstick skillet over medium heat. Lightly spritz with nonstick cooking spray and pour about ¼ cup of batter into the center of the pan. Quickly swirl the batter so that it coats the bottom of the pan. Cook the crepe for 30 seconds to 1 minute on the first side or until it's lightly golden on the bottom and the top is matte. Carefully flip the crepe and cook for another 15 to 30 seconds. Transfer the crepe to a plate and continue cooking until all the batter is used.

While the crepes cook, make the topping. Beat the mascarpone with the orange zest and 2 tablespoons of brown sugar. Add ¼ teaspoon of cinnamon and ½ teaspoon of vanilla and set aside.

continued

Place the crepe skillet back onto the heat and add the butter to melt. Add the berries and squeeze the orange juice overtop. Stir in the remaining 4 tablespoons of brown sugar and ¼ teaspoon of cinnamon and cook, stirring frequently, until the sugar dissolves and the blackberries burst and cook down slightly, about 2 minutes. Add the remaining 1 teaspoon vanilla and set aside.

Spread a dollop of the mascarpone mixture onto each crepe and spoon some of the warm blackberries overtop. Fold or roll up the crepes, and serve with more blackberries on the side.

Note:

Crepes can be made in advance and stored for up to 2 days in the fridge, or for up to 2 months if stacked, separated by wax or parchment paper, and stored in a tightly sealed container or zip-top bag in the freezer.

Veg & Starch

FAST
FLAVOR

FOOD
WASTE

ONE
POT-ISH

Pan con Tomate

SERVES 2 TO 4

4 thick slices ciabatta
   or sourdough

3 tablespoons extra virgin
   olive oil, divided

1 garlic clove

2 large ripe tomatoes, halved

Kosher or flaky sea salt

Freshly ground black pepper

Toppings such as fine herbs,
   anchovy fillets, olives, cured
   ham, crumbled cheese,
   chili flakes, etc.

This super simple Spanish dish, literally translated as "bread with tomato," is the perfect thing to make with ripe summer tomatoes. Serve for lunch, as a light dinner, or as a snack somewhere in between and top with whatever salty, herby, spicy things you have on hand.

Heat your broiler to high.

Arrange the bread on a sheet pan and drizzle with 1 tablespoon of the oil. Place the bread under the broiler until golden brown, 1 to 2 minutes, then flip and continue to toast for another minute or two until golden. Remove from the oven, cut the garlic clove in half, and rub the cut side of the garlic onto the hot toast. Set aside on serving plates.

Using the large holes of your box or cheese grater, grate the cut side of the tomatoes over a bowl. The pulpy flesh of the tomatoes will grate into a fresh tomato sauce, leaving the skins behind. Discard or save the skins for another use (see note).

Stir a tablespoon of the oil into the grated tomatoes and season well with salt and black pepper. Spoon the saucy tomatoes over the toast and garnish with whatever toppings you'd like. Drizzle over the remaining tablespoon of oil, season with salt and pepper, if needed, and serve immediately.

Note:

As with other vegetable scraps, tomato skins are a great addition to homemade vegetable broth (recipe on page 245). Store them in a zip-top bag along with other vegetable scraps and stash in the freezer until ready to use.

Irish Onion Soup

SERVES 4

3 tablespoons butter, divided

5–6 yellow onions, peeled and thinly sliced

Kosher salt

Freshly ground black pepper

1 tablespoon maple syrup

3 garlic cloves, finely grated

1 tablespoon finely chopped fresh sage

2 teaspoons finely chopped fresh thyme

1 fresh bay leaf, optional

2 tablespoons brandy

1 tablespoon balsamic vinegar

1 cup stout

4 cups beef broth

4 (½-inch thick) slices whole-grain bread or baguette, toasted

1⅓ cups grated extra-old white cheddar

Note:

If you don't have fresh herbs on hand, you can swap in dried ones. Just be sure to reduce the amount you're using, as dried herbs tend to have a more concentrated flavor. The general rule is 1 tablespoon of fresh herbs equals 1 teaspoon of dried herbs.

My Irish-inspired version of classic French onion soup uses budget-friendly pantry staples and about half a tallboy of stout, leaving the cook with a little tipple to have while the soup simmers. If stout isn't your beer of choice, you can use a lighter-bodied beer instead.

In a large saucepot over medium-low heat, melt 2 tablespoons of the butter. Add the onions and season with salt and pepper. Give the onions a stir and allow them to cook, stirring frequently, until softened and starting to brown slightly, about 15 minutes. Turn the heat up to medium, add the remaining butter and maple syrup, and continue to cook the onions until caramelized, about 10 minutes, stirring frequently. Turn the heat down to low, add the garlic, sage, thyme, and bay leaf, and cook for 30 seconds. Carefully deglaze the pan with the brandy and balsamic vinegar, stirring very well and scraping the bottom of the pan.

Add the stout and allow it to bubble until reduced by half, then stir in the beef broth and bring the mixture to a simmer. Reduce the heat to medium-low, cover the pot, and simmer for 25 to 30 minutes to allow the flavors to meld. Season the soup with more salt and pepper, if needed. At this point, you can cool the soup, transfer to containers, and store in the fridge for up to 3 days or in the freezer for up to 3 months.

When ready to serve, ladle the soup into four oven-safe ramekins or French onion soup dishes. If you don't have individual dishes, use a 9-inch round or square baking dish. Turn the broiler to high and top with the toast and grated cheese. Broil for 3 to 4 minutes until the cheese is golden brown and the soup is bubbling.

Allow to cool slightly before serving.

FAST
FLAVOR

FOOD
WASTE

ONE
POT-ISH

Green Ginger Miso Soup

SERVES 4

3 green onions, divided

1 small handful cilantro stalks, leaves reserved

½–1 green chili, such as a jalapeño or serrano, coarsely chopped

3 garlic cloves, smashed

4-inch piece fresh ginger, minced

3 tablespoons miso paste

1 tablespoon turmeric

1 teaspoon whole coriander seeds

2 limes, divided

1 tablespoon plus 1 teaspoon toasted sesame oil, divided

7 oz shiitake or cremini mushrooms, sliced

Kosher salt

Freshly ground black pepper

2 teaspoons soy sauce

4 cups low-sodium vegetable broth

8–9 oz soba noodles

3–4 handfuls dark leafy greens, coarsely chopped

1 lb medium or firm tofu, cut into bite-sized cubes

Miso paste is one of my favorite salty, savory flavor boosters. While it will last in your fridge for up to a year, it is best to use it within three months of opening for optimal flavor and freshness. Try adding a spoonful to homemade caramel, whip some into mashed potatoes, combine with butter or oil as a glaze on fish or meat, whisk some into your next homemade vinaigrette, or give my Miso Butter Corn Pasta a try (recipe on page 101). Here, I'm using it in a quick and hearty flavor-packed soup!

Coarsely chop two of the green onions along with the cilantro stalks and chili and add to the bowl of a food processor along with the garlic, ginger, miso paste, turmeric, and coriander seeds. Juice in one lime and add 1 tablespoon of sesame oil. Blitz to combine, adding a splash of water if needed to reach a thick pesto-y consistency. Set aside.

Place a large saucepan over medium heat and add 1 teaspoon of sesame oil. Add the mushrooms, season lightly with salt and pepper, and cook for 3 to 4 minutes or until golden brown. Stir in the soy sauce and then transfer the mushrooms to a plate and set aside.

Add the onion-miso mixture to the pan and cook for 30 seconds to 1 minute, until fragrant, then carefully pour in the broth. Turn the heat up to medium-high and bring to a boil. Once boiling, cook the soba noodles in the broth according to the package directions until al dente. Stir in the greens, tofu, and cooked mushrooms.

Thinly slice the remaining green onion and cut the remaining lime into quarters. Serve the soup scattered with the green onion and cilantro leaves, with a lime wedge on the side.

Note:

To extend the shelf life of your fresh ginger, store it in a zip-top bag in the freezer as soon as you get it home from the grocery store. Frozen ginger is a cinch to grate over a Microplane or rasp, and the freezing process softens the skin, removing the need to peel it before adding to a recipe.

Lemony Lentil Soup

SERVES 4 TO 6

FAST
FLAVOR

ONE
POT-ISH

PANTRY
STAPLES

2 tablespoons butter

1 yellow onion, finely diced

1 carrot, finely diced

Kosher salt

Freshly ground black pepper

2 yellow or green zucchinis,
thinly sliced

4 garlic cloves, thinly sliced

2 teaspoons turmeric

1 teaspoon cumin

¼ teaspoon cayenne pepper

1 cup red lentils

4 cups low-sodium vegetable
or chicken broth

2 lemons, zested and juiced

2 large handfuls dark leafy
greens, coarsely chopped

2 tablespoons chopped
parsley

2 tablespoons chopped mint,
plus more for serving

4–6 tablespoons sour cream
or yogurt

1½–2 oz crumbled feta,
optional

Unlike dried beans and peas, which benefit from a lengthy soak followed by a long cook, lentils cook up from dried in 15 to 40 minutes depending on the type. As such, lentils are what I reach for when I'm looking for a high-protein, quick-cooking vegetarian meal. With the bright flavors of lemon and herbs, this quick and easy soup is delicious served hot or cold.

Set a large saucepan over medium heat and melt the butter. Add the onion and carrot, season with salt and pepper, and cook until slightly softened, 3 to 4 minutes. Add the zucchinis, season with a little more salt and pepper, and cook for 5 minutes or until lightly golden brown.

Add the garlic and cook for 1 minute, then stir in the turmeric, cumin, cayenne, and lentils and toast, stirring frequently, for 1 minute.

Carefully pour in the broth along with 1 cup of water, turn the heat to high, and bring to a boil. Reduce the heat to medium and cook for 15 minutes, or until the lentils are tender.

Add the lemon zest and juice, greens, parsley, and mint, and season to taste with salt and pepper.

Serve the soup garnished with a dollop of sour cream, some fresh mint, and a scattering of feta.

Note:

When using dried pantry staples such as lentils or rice, I like to toast them in some oil or butter before adding any liquid. This gives a slightly toasty golden-brown flavor to the end result and helps freshen up dried ingredients that may have been sitting in my cupboards for longer than I'd care to admit.

Buffalo Roasted Cauliflower & Chickpea Pitas with Blue Cheese Slaw

SERVES 4 TO 5

2 tablespoons olive oil, divided

½ cup all-purpose flour

¼ cup cornstarch

1½ teaspoons garlic powder

1 teaspoon smoked paprika

1 teaspoon cayenne pepper

½ teaspoon cumin

1 teaspoon kosher salt

¾ cup soda water or light-flavored beer

½ head cauliflower, cut into small florets

1 can (19 fl oz) chickpeas, drained, rinsed, and dried

1 cup panko breadcrumbs

¾ cup cayenne pepper hot sauce, such as Frank's RedHot

3 tablespoons melted butter

FOR SERVING

2 tablespoons mayonnaise

¼ cup sour cream or Greek yogurt

½ lemon, juiced

1 tablespoon white vinegar

½ teaspoon Dijon mustard

½ teaspoon garlic powder

½ cup crumbled blue cheese

Kosher salt

Freshly ground black pepper

2 tablespoons finely chopped chives

1 carrot, peeled and shredded

4 stalks celery, thinly sliced, leaves reserved

4–5 pitas, Greek or pocket

One of my great food obsessions is Frank's RedHot sauce. Sure, other hot sauces are great, and there are certain things that can only be paired with Tabasco, but Frank's is my ride or die. While filming my television show *Mary Makes It Easy*, I mentioned this love enough times to warrant my wonderful friend and producer Michelle tracking down and buying me *literally* the biggest jug of the stuff as a wrap gift. The jug was one gallon, made for restaurants. It didn't even last the year.

Preheat your oven to 450°F and drizzle 1 tablespoon of the oil onto a sheet pan.

In a large bowl, combine the flour, cornstarch, garlic powder, smoked paprika, cayenne pepper, cumin, and salt and whisk to combine. Whisk in the soda water, then add the cauliflower florets and chickpeas. Stir well to evenly coat the cauliflower and chickpeas in the batter.

Add the breadcrumbs to a separate large bowl. Dump the cauliflower and chickpeas into the panko and toss very well to combine and evenly coat, then transfer the cauliflower and chickpeas to the prepared sheet pan. Spread into an even layer, leaving some room between each piece. Drizzle over the remaining tablespoon of oil and bake for 25 to 30 minutes until golden and crisp, tossing halfway through.

Meanwhile, make the buffalo sauce by whisking the hot sauce and butter together. Remove the cauliflower and chickpeas from the oven and toss with the buffalo sauce. Return to the oven for 5 minutes to allow the sauce to soak in.

While the cauliflower and chickpeas cook, whisk the mayonnaise, sour cream, lemon juice, vinegar, mustard, and garlic powder together in a large bowl. Stir in the blue cheese and season with salt and pepper. Stir in the chives, carrot, and celery, reserving the leaves for garnish.

Note:

Cornstarch is one of my favorite savory and sweet secret weapons in the kitchen. It can be used to thicken simmering sauces and gravies or baked fruit fillings, and it also adds super crispiness to baked and fried coatings.

Stuff the pitas with the buffalo cauliflower and chickpeas and top with the blue cheese slaw. Scatter with the reserved celery leaves and serve.

Leftover cauliflower and chickpeas can be stored in the fridge for up to 3 days.

Black Bean Chipotle Veggie Burger

SERVES 6

1½ cups (4 oz) coarsely
    chopped mushrooms

Kosher salt

4 teaspoons olive oil, divided

1 onion, diced

Freshly ground black pepper

2 garlic cloves, coarsely
    chopped

1½ teaspoons cumin

½ teaspoon smoked paprika

1–2 tablespoons chipotle
    peppers in adobo sauce
    (see note on page 12)

1 cup walnut halves

2 cups (about 1 can) black
    beans, drained and rinsed

1 cup cooked rice

1 egg

1 tablespoon Dijon mustard

1–2 tablespoons plain
    breadcrumbs

6 cheese slices, optional

6 hamburger buns, toasted

Classic burger toppings

I've made and eaten my fair share of veggie burgers in my time and, let me tell you, some are horrible. You know the ones I'm talking about. They are basically just weird hot hummus patties hiding under toppings, in between a bun, masquerading as something delicious. With the combination of mushrooms, rice, beans, and walnuts in these veggie burgers and the multi-step food processor method, you don't have to worry about making a sad veggie burger ever again.

Heat a large nonstick skillet over medium heat. Add the mushrooms to the dry pan, season with salt, and cook for 5 minutes or until some of the moisture cooks out and the mushrooms begin to caramelize. Add 2 teaspoons of oil along with the onion, season with salt and pepper, and cook until golden brown, 4 to 5 minutes. Stir in the garlic, cumin, and paprika, and cook for 1 to 2 minutes. Transfer to the bowl of a food processor along with the chipotles, to taste.

Place the skillet back over medium heat. Add the walnuts to toast for 1 to 2 minutes until nutty smelling, stirring frequently. Transfer to the food processor and pulse with the mushroom mixture until finely chopped. Scrape into a large bowl and set aside.

Add the black beans and rice to the food processor and pulse two to four times to coarsely chop and combine. Add to the mushroom mixture along with the egg, mustard, 1 tablespoon of breadcrumbs, ½ teaspoon of salt, and ¼ teaspoon of pepper. Stir well to evenly combine. If the mixture is a little loose or too sticky to handle, add the other tablespoon of breadcrumbs.

Place the nonstick skillet over medium-high heat and add the remaining 2 teaspoons of oil. Divide the mixture into six equal pieces, about ½ cup each, and shape into burgers roughly the size of your buns. Flatter patties will be generally firmer and crispier. Thicker patties will have a nice crisp exterior with a more tender center.

Cook until golden brown, 3 to 4 minutes per side. If making cheeseburgers, add a slice of cheese to each patty, cover the pan with a lid, and allow the cheese to melt for about 1 minute. Serve the patties on toasted buns with your favorite toppings.

Note:

Despite their appearance, mushrooms hold a lot of water. By starting them in a dry pan, you can quickly cook out that water, concentrating the mushroom flavor, and making them easier to cook and caramelize without the risk of steaming.

Crispy Garlic Parmesan Potatoes with Roasted Garlic Mayo

SERVES 4

FAST
FLAVOR

ONE
POT-ISH

PANTRY
STAPLE

1 head garlic

4 tablespoons olive oil, divided

Kosher salt

Freshly ground black pepper

¾ cup ground Parmigiano-Reggiano cheese

¼ cup plain breadcrumbs

½ teaspoon garlic powder

½ teaspoon dried Italian seasoning

2 lb mini potatoes

½ cup mayonnaise

2 tablespoons finely chopped parsley, divided

Note:

Whenever a recipe I've written calls for ground Parmigiano-Reggiano cheese as opposed to grated, you'll want to use either the ground stuff you get in little tubs in the deli section of your grocery store or go with my lifelong staple: a can of shaky cheese (often simply labeled "Parmesan"). It is my favorite budget-friendly ingredient that I use regularly to get parm flavor into crispy coatings without the risk of burning.

I don't know why, but potatoes rarely make their way onto my table midweek—they always seem to be associated with dinner parties or the holidays. But now, with a recipe like this, fancy shindig-worthy potatoes can be a thing any night I want.

Preheat your oven to 425°F.

Cut off the top of the garlic so that the cloves are exposed and place on a square of aluminum foil. Drizzle with 1 tablespoon of oil and season with salt and pepper. Wrap the garlic in the foil and roast for 15 minutes.

Meanwhile, drizzle 2 tablespoons of the oil into a 9-by-13-inch baking pan and tip and tilt the pan to ensure the bottom is coated in the oil.

In a small bowl, combine the Parmigiano-Reggiano, breadcrumbs, garlic powder, and Italian seasoning, along with ½ teaspoon of salt and ¼ teaspoon of pepper. Evenly scatter into the prepared baking pan, shaking the pan to create an even layer.

Cut the mini potatoes in half and transfer them to the pan, cut side down. Drizzle the top with the remaining 1 tablespoon of oil and transfer to the oven alongside the garlic. Roast for 25 minutes, without flipping, or until the potatoes are golden brown and fork tender and the garlic is soft.

Set the potatoes aside to rest in the pan for 5 minutes. Meanwhile, unwrap the roasted garlic and squeeze as much of it as you'd like into the mayonnaise. Store any leftover garlic tightly wrapped in the fridge for another use for up to 2 weeks. Add 1 tablespoon of parsley to the mayo and mix well to combine.

Using a spatula, transfer the potatoes onto a serving dish, scatter with the remaining parsley, and serve with the roasted garlic mayonnaise.

ONE
POT-ISH

PANTRY
STAPLE

SIMPLY
SNAZZY

Spicy Roasted Sweet Potatoes

SERVES 4

3 tablespoons olive oil, divided

2 teaspoons honey

1½ teaspoons cumin

½ teaspoon kosher salt

4 teaspoons finely chopped chipotle peppers in adobo sauce, divided

1½ lb sweet potatoes, peeled or scrubbed

½ cup sour cream

1 lemon or lime, halved

1 green onion, thinly sliced

1 small handful cilantro, coarsely chopped

I'm a big fan of flavorful veg that can act as either a side or as the substantial part of a vegetarian main. These spicy sweet potatoes make a great accompaniment to any meal that could do with a bit of a kick and work amazingly as the main filling for vegetarian tacos.

Preheat your oven to 425°F and drizzle 1 tablespoon of oil on a large baking sheet.

In a large bowl, whisk the remaining 2 tablespoons of oil with the honey, cumin, salt, and 2 teaspoons of chipotles.

Cut the sweet potatoes into large chunks and add to the bowl. Toss well to evenly coat, then transfer to the prepared baking sheet.

Roast for 30 to 35 minutes or until the potatoes are tender and caramelized, tossing halfway through.

Meanwhile, in a small bowl, combine the sour cream, remaining 2 teaspoons of chipotles, and the juice of half of the lemon. Season with salt and set aside.

Remove the potatoes from the oven and, while still hot, squeeze over the juice from the remaining half lemon. Scatter the green onions and cilantro overtop and serve immediately with chipotle sour cream.

Note:

Don't throw out your old, dull, and battered sheet pans. They brown vegetables and meat better than their shiny new counterparts, which are better suited to baking.

Green Couscous Salad

SERVES 6 TO 8

FAST
FLAVOR

FOOD
WASTE

GET
AHEAD

FOR THE DILL SAUCE

1 handful baby spinach
   or arugula

½ cup lightly packed dill

½ cup lightly packed parsley

1 garlic clove

1 lemon, zested and juiced

1 teaspoon Dijon mustard

2½ oz goat cheese or feta

¼ cup plain yogurt

Kosher salt

Freshly ground black pepper

FOR THE SALAD

1 tablespoon olive oil

1½ cups Israeli couscous

3 cups low-sodium vegetable
   broth

Kosher salt

Freshly ground black pepper

1 English cucumber, diced

1 avocado, diced

3 green onions, thinly sliced

½ cup coarsely chopped
   parsley

½ cup coarsely chopped dill

2½ oz goat cheese or feta,
   crumbled

One of the biggest issues I hear from home cooks is that the herbs they buy always seem to go bad before they can use them. I get it! Who hasn't opened their crisper to find that forgotten bag of muck formerly known as cilantro? With this simple prep-ahead recipe, bunches of fresh herbs pull double duty acting as both the lettuce stand-in for the salad itself and as the base of a bright and herby sauce that would also be great spooned over seared or grilled fish.

For the dill sauce, in a food processor or blender, combine the baby spinach with the dill, parsley, garlic, lemon zest, lemon juice, mustard, goat cheese, and yogurt. Blitz into a smooth sauce, then season to taste with salt and pepper. Pour into a large bowl and set aside.

For the salad, place a medium saucepan over medium heat. Add the oil and couscous and cook, stirring frequently, for 1 to 2 minutes or until lightly toasted and nutty smelling.

Carefully add the vegetable broth, season with salt and pepper, and bring to a boil over medium-high heat. Reduce the heat to a simmer, cover, and cook for 10 minutes. Remove the pot from the heat and leave covered for 5 minutes to allow the couscous to absorb the liquid. Set aside to cool slightly or all the way to room temperature.

Add the cucumber, avocado, and green onions to the sauce along with the parsley and dill. Pour over the cooled couscous and stir well to combine. Season to taste with salt and pepper and serve scattered with the goat cheese.

The salad will keep in the fridge for up to 3 days.

Note:

Israeli couscous is actually a small cut of pasta. If you cannot find it at your local grocery store, you can substitute orzo or acini di pepe.

Fried Feta Salad with Honey & Herbs

SERVES 4

¼ cup all-purpose flour

1 egg

½ cup panko breadcrumbs

Freshly ground black pepper

Kosher salt

7 oz block feta, diced into
   1-inch cubes

¼ cup olive oil

1 lemon, zested and juiced

1 garlic clove, finely grated

2 teaspoons Dijon mustard

1 teaspoon + 1 tablespoon
   honey, divided

3 tablespoons extra virgin
   olive oil

4–5 handfuls arugula or
   baby gem lettuce

2–3 tablespoons chopped
   herbs, such as basil, parsley,
   chives, oregano, thyme, or
   rosemary

This is basically just a grown-up, saltier version of mozzarella sticks served on crisp greens, and there is absolutely nothing wrong with that. By changing the herbs from fine to woody, this salad goes from a plate of spring and summer freshness to the perfect first course in a cold-weather feast.

Set out three shallow bowls or plates and add the flour into one, whisk the egg in another, and scatter the breadcrumbs into the third. Season each with pepper and a little bit of salt—remember, feta is quite salty. Dredge the feta cubes in the flour, then transfer to the egg and turn to coat, allowing any excess egg to drip off. Press the feta into the breadcrumbs to evenly coat, transfer to a small baking sheet, and place in the freezer for 10 to 30 minutes.

To fry the feta, place a skillet over medium heat and add the ¼ cup olive oil. When the oil is hot, retrieve the cheese from the freezer and cook for 2 to 3 minutes per side or until golden brown.

Meanwhile, prepare the salad by whisking the lemon zest, lemon juice, garlic, Dijon mustard, and 1 teaspoon of honey together. While whisking, slowly stream in the extra virgin olive oil and season with salt and pepper. Add the arugula, toss to combine, and transfer to a serving dish.

Add the crispy fried feta onto the salad and drizzle with the remaining honey. Scatter with herbs, season with pepper, and serve immediately.

Note:

If you're looking to really impress with your next cheese board, keep the brick of feta whole and prepare as above, leaving out the salad. Serve as-is, drizzled with honey, scattered with herbs, and seasoned with pepper alongside your favorite crackers or crostini.

Romaine & Endive Salad with Anchovy Lemon Dressing & Crispy Breadcrumbs

SERVES 4 TO 6

FAST FLAVOR

FOOD WASTE

GET AHEAD

¼ cup mayonnaise

2 teaspoons Dijon mustard

1 lemon, zested and juiced

3 anchovy fillets, very finely minced

1 tablespoon capers, finely chopped

2 garlic cloves, finely grated, divided

½ cup finely grated pecorino, divided

Freshly ground black pepper

1 head Belgian endive

1 romaine heart or 2 heads baby gem lettuce

1 tablespoon olive oil

2 slices stale bread, torn into small pieces

Kosher salt

1 tablespoon finely chopped parsley

Even in all the excitement of buying and moving into our first home, there were some bittersweet feelings involved. Aaron and I loved our old neighborhood and, having lived there for 10 years, we had our spots. We knew where to go for a quick bite, a good pint of beer, cheap diner breakfasts, and, most importantly, we had our go-to date night spot. Luckily, within the first few days of moving, we found our new place. This is my attempt at the rich and creamy lemon anchovy dressing and crispy breadcrumb topper that adorns our new favorite salad.

In a large bowl, whisk together the mayonnaise, mustard, lemon zest, lemon juice, anchovies, capers, and 1 clove of garlic. Whisk in ¼ cup of the pecorino and season with lots of black pepper.

Trim the ends off the endive and lettuce and separate the leaves. Add them to the bowl of dressing and set aside.

Place a large skillet over medium heat. Add the oil and bread pieces and cook, stirring and tossing frequently, until golden and crisp, 3 to 4 minutes. Stir in the remaining garlic, season with salt and pepper, and cook for another minute to take the raw edge off the garlic. Add the remaining pecorino and cook for 30 seconds to crisp the cheese. Stir in the parsley and set aside.

Toss the salad well, then serve scattered with the breadcrumbs.

The dressing and breadcrumbs can be made up to 3 days in advance. Transfer both to airtight containers and store the dressing in the fridge and the breadcrumbs at room temperature.

Note:

For a creamy vegan version of this or really any Caesar-ish dressing, use 2 tablespoons of tahini, 2 tablespoons of oil, and a splash of water instead of the mayo and leave out the anchovies and pecorino altogether. The tahini will give a nice savory funkiness that works well to replace the funk of pecorino and the umami of anchovies.

Bistro Salad

SERVES 4 TO 6

FAST FLAVOR

GET AHEAD

3 tablespoons white wine vinegar

1 garlic clove, finely grated

1 anchovy fillet, finely minced, optional

1 tablespoon Dijon mustard, preferably stone ground

2 teaspoons maple syrup

½ teaspoon herbes de Provence or dried thyme

¼ cup + 1 tablespoon extra virgin olive oil, divided

Kosher salt

Freshly ground black pepper

1 shallot, thinly sliced

10–11 oz mini potatoes, halved

4 eggs

7 oz green beans, trimmed

7 oz yellow beans, trimmed

There are two categories of food my mom refuses to eat: pink foods and squeaky foods. Outside of strawberry ice cream and cotton candy, the first hasn't caused many issues, but her aversion to "squeaky" food can be a bit of a pain when I'm trying to plan dinner. The number-one ingredient on the squeaky food list is green beans, but I argue that their squeakiness can be replaced by crispness if cooked properly. By blanching them just until they are bright in color then plunging them into an ice bath, the beans in this lettuce-free salad get that coveted Myra Berg seal of approval.

In a large bowl, whisk together the vinegar, garlic, anchovy, Dijon, maple syrup, and herbes de Provence. While whisking, slowly stream in ¼ cup of oil. Season to taste with salt and pepper and stir in the shallot. Set aside to allow the shallot to marinate while you prepare the rest of the ingredients.

Add the potatoes to a large pot and cover with cold water. Season well with salt and bring to a boil over high heat. Cook the potatoes until fork tender, 10 to 12 minutes depending on the size of your potatoes. Using a slotted spoon, scoop the potatoes from the boiling water and add to the dressing and shallots. Toss to combine and set aside.

Carefully lower the eggs into the boiling water, turn the heat down to medium-low, and cook the eggs for 7 minutes for a jammy center. While the eggs cook, prepare an ice bath with a few cups of ice and cold water in a large bowl. Transfer the eggs to the ice bath and allow them to cool for about 3 minutes or until cool enough to touch.

Turn the heat under the pot back up to high and season with another pinch of salt. Add the beans to blanch for 1 to 2 minutes or until bright in color but still crisp. Drain the beans and add to the ice bath for 15 seconds to stop the cooking process and lock in the color and crisp texture.

continued

Remove the beans from the ice bath and add to the potatoes, shallots, and dressing. Toss well to combine and evenly coat all the vegetables, then season to taste with salt and pepper.

Transfer to a serving dish, peel and halve the boiled eggs, and drizzle the remaining tablespoon of oil overtop. Season with more salt and pepper and serve.

This salad is delicious served warm or cold. It will keep in the fridge for up to 3 days, though the beans will lose some of their vivid color due to the vinegary dressing.

Note:

The emulsifying power of things like mustard and egg yolks are pretty well known, but did you know that maple syrup also helps opposites attract? Adding a splash of maple syrup to your next batch of vinaigrette will not only add a bit of sweetness but also help keep the oil and vinegar from separating.

Eggplant Parmesan

SERVES 4 TO 6

2 medium eggplants

2 eggs

¼ cup mayonnaise

1½ cups ground Parmigiano-Reggiano cheese, plus more for serving

1¼ cups panko breadcrumbs

1½ teaspoons dried Italian seasoning

1 teaspoon garlic powder

Kosher salt

Freshly ground black pepper

2 tablespoons olive oil, plus more for frying

1 pint cherry tomatoes, halved

2 garlic cloves, finely grated

1 can (27 fl oz) crushed tomatoes

2 tablespoons finely chopped parsley

2 tablespoons finely chopped basil

1 tablespoon finely chopped oregano

½ teaspoon crushed red pepper flakes

8 oz ball fresh mozzarella, thinly sliced

Top anything with tomato sauce and cheese, and I'm on board, but chicken parm holds a special place in my food memories. For my sixteenth birthday dinner, my mom made a huge pan of the most delicious chicken parm ever. I think about that meal so often that I wanted to be able to revisit it whenever I wanted. As I no longer eat chicken, eggplant is the perfect substitute. It's juicy, meaty, and crisp and provides a great base for a flavorful, quick sauce and a whole lot of melty mozzarella.

Preheat your oven to 400°F. Trim the stem and bottom from each eggplant and slice into ¾-inch-thick rounds.

In a shallow dish, beat together the eggs and mayonnaise. In a separate shallow dish, combine the ground Parmigiano-Reggiano cheese, breadcrumbs, Italian seasoning, garlic powder, and ½ teaspoon each of salt and pepper. Working with one piece of eggplant at a time, dip it into the egg mixture to coat then toss in the breadcrumb mixture, pressing firmly to make the breadcrumbs stick. Set aside.

When all the eggplant is coated, place a large cast-iron skillet or oven-safe sauté pan over medium-high heat. Add the oil and swirl to coat the bottom of the pan. Working in batches to avoid overcrowding the pan, cook the eggplant for 2 to 3 minutes per side or until golden brown, adjusting the heat as necessary. Remove to a plate and continue to cook the eggplant, adding more oil to the pan as needed.

Once the eggplant has all been browned, turn the heat down to medium and add a splash of oil to the pan. Add the cherry tomatoes, season with salt and pepper, and cook for 2 to 3 minutes just until they start to break down and get juicy. Stir in the garlic and cook for 30 seconds. Remove the pan from the heat and transfer the cherry tomatoes and garlic to a large bowl or a 4-cup glass measuring cup. Stir in the crushed tomatoes, parsley, basil, oregano, and red pepper flakes. Season to taste with salt and pepper.

continued

Spread about 1 cup of the sauce into the bottom of the skillet or sauté pan and layer in the eggplant, topping each slice with a spoonful of sauce before layering with cheese and more eggplant. Continue until all the eggplant is used up. I like to layer mine on an angle as I find that keeps the eggplant a little crisper.

Transfer the pan to the oven and bake for 20 to 25 minutes or until the cheese is melted and golden brown.

Allow the eggplant Parmesan to cool for 5 minutes before serving scattered with more fresh herbs and Parmigiano-Reggiano cheese, if desired.

Note:

If you prefer or just happen to have it on hand, substitute regular low-moisture mozzarella, sometimes called pizza mozzarella, for the fresh mozzarella.

Creamed Corn Baked Feta

SERVES 4 TO 6

FAST
FLAVOR

ONE
POT-ISH

PANTRY
STAPLES

1 tablespoon butter

1 small red or yellow onion, finely diced

Kosher salt

Freshly ground black pepper

1 garlic clove, finely grated

2 teaspoons all-purpose flour

¾ cup warm milk

½ cup cream

1½ teaspoons sugar

3½ cups corn kernels, fresh, frozen, or canned

1 block (7 oz) feta cheese

¼ cup finely chopped chives

2 tablespoons finely chopped parsley

I don't typically buy into new trends sight unseen, as I'm a lifelong fan of the classics. That being said, when that baked feta situation was making its rounds on the internet, oooh baby, was my interest piqued. To jump on that culinary bandwagon while staying true to my love of retro, I give you the most deliciously passé recipe I could think of with that creamy, dreamy baked feta goodness.

Heat a cast-iron or oven-safe skillet over medium heat. Add the butter and onion, season with salt and pepper, and cook until lightly golden brown, about 5 minutes.

Add the garlic and cook for 30 seconds. Sprinkle over the flour, whisk it in, and cook for another 30 seconds to 1 minute. While whisking, slowly pour in the milk followed by the cream. Add the sugar and bring the mixture to a simmer. Cook for 2 to 3 minutes, stirring occasionally, until slightly thickened.

Set your oven rack to the center position and turn the broiler to high.

Stir in the corn and allow it to cook for 4 to 5 minutes or until tender. Roughly crumble the feta overtop and transfer to the oven for 5 to 7 minutes or until the feta is golden brown.

Remove the pan from the oven, scatter over the chives and parsley, season with more pepper and salt, if needed, and stir well to combine.

Serve immediately.

Note:

For the creamiest feta, look for varieties that boast a higher concentration of sheep's milk. The more goat or cow milk used, the crumblier the feta, which, while good for salads, won't melt as well.

Caramelized Shallots with Sherry Vinegar & Pistachios

SERVES 4

ONE
POT-ISH

PANTRY
STAPLE

SIMPLY
SNAZZY

1 tablespoon olive oil

8–10 sage leaves

Kosher salt

2 tablespoons butter

8 medium shallots, peeled
and halved

Freshly ground black pepper

2 tablespoons packed
brown sugar

3 tablespoons sherry vinegar

¼ cup salted pistachios,
coarsely chopped

Alliums like onions, leeks, and shallots are often relegated to the role of a supporting act, but if you've never given them the chance to shine as the star of the show, you are missing out. These simple, very French-feeling sweet and tangy shallots are the perfect side to your next Sunday roast or even served alongside a wedge of brie as a snazzy app.

Preheat your oven to 375°F and place a cast-iron or oven-safe skillet over medium heat.

Add the oil, and when it's hot, carefully sprinkle in the sage leaves to fry. They will sizzle and crisp up in 10 to 15 seconds. Remove the sage to a piece of paper towel, sprinkle immediately with salt, and set aside.

Add the butter into the pan to melt. Toss in the shallots, season with salt and pepper, and cook, gently stirring and tossing occasionally, for 4 to 5 minutes or until beginning to caramelize. Gently stir in the sugar and, standing slightly back from your stove to avoid the steam, stir in the vinegar. Arrange the shallots in a single layer and transfer to the oven for 20 to 25 minutes until fork tender and well caramelized.

Transfer to a bowl or serve in the pan scattered with the chopped pistachios and fried sage leaves.

Note:

Shallots have a delicate, sweet onion flavor with a hint of sharpness, kind of like if a red onion and a clove of garlic had a baby. If you can't find shallots at your grocery store or just don't feel like picking any up during your next shop, you can swap four red onions cut into thick wedges and a couple of whole garlic cloves for a similar flavor profile.

Parmesan Zucchini with Crispy Chickpeas & Tahini Ricotta

SERVES 4 TO 6 AS A SIDE, 2 TO 3 AS A MAIN

2 zucchinis, trimmed

4 teaspoons olive oil or
    sun-dried tomato oil, divided

Kosher salt

Freshly ground black pepper

⅓ cup ground Parmigiano-
    Reggiano cheese

1 can (19 fl oz) chickpeas,
    drained and rinsed

¼ cup oil-packed sun-dried
    tomatoes, finely chopped

2 garlic cloves, divided

½ cup ricotta cheese

3 tablespoons tahini

1 lemon, zested and juiced

2 teaspoons finely chopped
    parsley, plus more for serving

1 teaspoon finely chopped
    oregano, plus more for serving

Sun-dried tomato oil,
    for drizzling

One of my mom's go-to side dishes, roasted Parmesan zucchini, is a staple for a reason. It's simple, straightforward, and delicious. To give it a bit of an update, I've added savory crispy chickpeas and tahini ricotta. This dish easily doubles as a delicious side and filling vegetarian main.

Preheat your oven to 425°F.

Cut the zucchinis in half lengthwise, then cut on the diagonal into ½-inch-thick slices. Transfer the sliced zucchini to a baking sheet and drizzle with 2 teaspoons of the oil. Season with salt and pepper and roast for 5 to 7 minutes, until slightly tender. Toss the zucchini, then scatter the Parmigiano-Reggiano cheese on top. Return to the oven, turn the broiler to high, and broil for 2 to 3 minutes until the cheese is golden brown. Set aside.

Place a large skillet over medium heat. Add the remaining 2 teaspoons of oil to the skillet along with the chickpeas. Season with salt and pepper and cook for 5 to 6 minutes or until lightly golden and crisp, stirring frequently. Add the sun-dried tomatoes, grate in one garlic clove, and stir to combine. Turn the heat down to low to keep warm.

Meanwhile, stir together the ricotta, tahini, lemon zest, lemon juice, parsley, and oregano. Grate in the remaining garlic clove and season to taste with salt and pepper.

To serve, spread the ricotta mixture onto a large serving dish or four individual dishes. Top with the chickpeas and zucchini. Drizzle with some oil from the sun-dried tomatoes and garnish with some parsley and oregano.

Note:

While delicious served hot, this recipe is just as good cold and is a dream as part of a picnic spread. All elements can be made in advance and stored in the fridge for up to 3 days.

Balsamic Grilled Radicchio & Pears

SERVES 4 TO 6

FAST
FLAVOR

ONE
POT-ISH

2–3 heads radicchio

2 Anjou or Bosc pears

4–6 slices prosciutto, optional

2 tablespoons olive oil

Kosher salt

Freshly ground black pepper

2 tablespoons balsamic
  vinegar

⅓ cup pesto, store-bought
  or see recipe on page 246

4½ oz crumbled goat cheese

¼ cup shelled pistachios

1 small handful basil leaves

Up until a few years ago, I wasn't a huge fan of chicories. It's not that I didn't like them per se but the slightly bitter flavor of these crisp lettuce-like vegetables always came as a shock when I'd encounter them in salads. It wasn't until I tried grilling radicchio that I started coming around to the wonders of these beautiful red heads. Grilling them softens their texture along with their bitterness, giving them a sweet flavor that pairs perfectly with balsamic vinegar.

Cut each head of radicchio into four or six wedges through the root. Peel, quarter, and core the pears. Transfer to a plate or small baking sheet along with the prosciutto and drizzle with the oil, tossing to evenly coat. Season with salt and pepper and set aside.

Heat your grill or a grill pan to medium. Add the radicchio, pears, and prosciutto to the grill. Cook, turning occasionally, until the prosciutto is crisp, 2 to 3 minutes, and the radicchio and pears are charred, 5 to 8 minutes. Transfer the crispy prosciutto to a cutting board and allow to cool slightly before chopping into bite-sized pieces. Place the radicchio and pears back onto the plate and drizzle with the vinegar.

Spread the pesto onto the bottom of a serving plate and top with the radicchio and pears. Scatter the goat cheese, pistachios, crispy prosciutto, and basil leaves overtop, and serve.

Note:

For a slightly less sharp vinegary taste, toss the radicchio, pears, and prosciutto with the balsamic vinegar before grilling. The heat of the grill will cook away the acidity, giving the final dish a sweeter flavor.

Smoky Harissa Eggplant
with Herby Feta Oil & Pine Nuts

SERVES 4 AS A SIDE, 2 AS A MAIN

1 large eggplant

Kosher salt

2 tablespoons harissa paste

4 tablespoons olive oil, divided

Freshly ground black pepper

2 oz crumbled feta cheese

1 lemon, zested

2 tablespoons finely chopped
    mint

2 tablespoons finely chopped
    parsley

2 teaspoons finely chopped
    oregano

2 tablespoons pine nuts

Note:

Harissa is a Tunisian spice blend that brings spicy and smoky flavor to anything you add it to. It's a great addition to any pantry, and, while delicious with fish and meat, I particularly love adding it to veg dishes, from soups and eggs to salad dressings and roasted veg.

Bitter things are great. Walnuts, dark chocolate, Campari, coffee, tahini, Alanis Morissette's 1995 seminal album *Jagged Little Pill*—I could go on! But rather than do that, I'm here to tell you that there's one ingredient often treated as bitter that just plain isn't: eggplant. Over the years, farmers and seed producers have bred out the bitterness that eggplants once had, leaving us with sweet, tender fruits perfect for roasting, grilling, sautéing, and frying. While they are no longer bitter, salting eggplant before cooking is still a beneficial step. It helps remove excess moisture to concentrate flavor and improve the overall texture.

Preheat your oven to 425°F.

Prepare the eggplant by trimming off the stem and quartering it lengthwise. Using the tip of a knife, lightly score the cut sides in a crosshatch pattern and transfer to a baking sheet. Sprinkle the eggplant with salt and leave for 20 minutes to draw out some of the moisture.

In a small bowl, combine the harissa with 1 tablespoon of the oil. Wipe the eggplant with a piece of paper towel to remove any moisture and excess salt. Brush the harissa mixture onto the eggplant and season with a little salt and pepper.

Roast the eggplant, without flipping, for 25 to 30 minutes or until golden and tender.

Meanwhile, in a small bowl, mix the remaining 3 tablespoons of oil with the feta, lemon zest, mint, parsley, and oregano. Season with pepper and set aside.

Place a small skillet over medium heat and toast the pine nuts until lightly golden, about 2 minutes. Transfer the toasted nuts to a bowl.

Transfer the roasted eggplant to a serving dish, spoon the herby feta oil overtop, and scatter with pine nuts. Serve hot or at room temperature.

Roasted Mushrooms with Blue Cheese Rosemary Crumb

SERVES 4

3 garlic cloves, finely chopped

2 tablespoons sherry or balsamic vinegar

1 tablespoon grainy Dijon mustard

2 teaspoons maple syrup

4 tablespoons olive oil, divided

3 sprigs rosemary, divided

Kosher salt

Freshly ground black pepper

1 lb mixed mushrooms, cleaned and stems trimmed

2–3 slices whole-grain bread

2½ oz crumbled blue cheese

Stuffed mushrooms are a steakhouse classic. They're typically made with buttons, creminis, or portobellos, as their cupped caps lend themselves well to filling, but go with whatever fancy fungus is in season or looks good at the market. These mushrooms are delicious as a side or spooned on top of grilled steak.

Preheat your oven to 425°F.

In a large bowl, whisk together the garlic, vinegar, mustard, maple syrup, and 3 tablespoons of the oil. Strip the leaves from one sprig of rosemary and finely chop. Add half of the chopped rosemary to the bowl along with the remaining two full sprigs. Season with salt and pepper, then add the mushrooms. Toss well to combine and transfer the mushrooms, gill side down, to a baking sheet.

Roast the mushrooms for 10 minutes.

Meanwhile, using your fingers, tear the bread into small pieces. Add to the large bowl along with the blue cheese and remaining chopped rosemary and tablespoon of oil. Season with salt and pepper.

Remove the mushrooms from the oven, stir, and scatter the bread mixture overtop. Return to the oven and roast for 10 to 15 minutes or until the mushrooms are cooked down and golden and the topping is crisp.

Serve immediately.

Note:

When roasting or grilling mushrooms, especially wide-capped mushrooms like portobellos, start them gill side down. This will stop moisture from pooling in the cap, allowing their flavor to concentrate.

Green Veg Gratin

SERVES 6

2 medium bunches dark
   leafy greens, baby broccoli,
   or rapini

1 tablespoon butter

1 yellow onion, finely diced

Kosher salt

Freshly ground black pepper

4 garlic cloves, thinly sliced

1 cup 35% whipping cream

1 teaspoon herbes de Provence

½ teaspoon freshly grated
   nutmeg

½ lemon, zested and juiced

5 oz Gruyère or Swiss cheese,
   grated

½ cup panko breadcrumbs

½ teaspoon crushed red
   pepper flakes

1 tablespoon olive oil

Note:

While you might want to
cut corners with the dairy
in this recipe, when adding
something acidic like lemon
juice to cream, a high fat
percentage is necessary
to keep it from curdling.

We all know that we should eat more greens. Well, that is everyone who isn't my friend Veronica. After meeting and living together while filming *MasterChef Canada*, I quickly realized that my new friend is a green-eating machine. Seriously, the amount of green leafy veg that she eats in a week would have lasted me for longer than I care to admit. Since then, I make a point of adding a handful of greens to pretty much anything that can handle it. Getting more greens in any way you can—even doused in cream and cheese—is always a good thing.

Preheat your oven to 350°F.

Prepare the greens by trimming or removing any of the tough stalks or stems. Wash the greens in cold water and shake gently to remove most of the water.

Set a large cast-iron or oven-safe sauté pan over medium heat. Melt the butter, add the onion, and season with salt and pepper. Cook for 4 to 5 minutes until the onion is tender and lightly golden brown. Stir in the garlic and cook for an additional 30 seconds. Working in batches, add the greens, season with salt and pepper, and cook just to wilt down slightly, about 1 minute per batch, before transferring the wilted greens to a plate.

Add the cream into the pan along with the herbes de Provence and nutmeg. Bring the cream to a simmer and cook down for about 5 minutes to slightly reduce and bring the flavors together.

Add the greens back into the pan along with the lemon zest and juice, stirring well to combine. Remove from the heat and scatter the cheese overtop. In a small bowl, stir together the breadcrumbs, red pepper flakes, and oil, season with salt and pepper, and scatter over the greens.

Bake the gratin for 30 to 35 minutes or until bubbling and the top is golden brown. Set aside to rest for 5 minutes before serving.

Pan-Fried Halloumi with Greens & Romesco

SERVES 4

FAST
FLAVOR

PANTRY
STAPLES

¼ cup coarsely chopped almonds

3 garlic cloves, divided

1½ cups (about 12 oz) jarred roasted red peppers, drained

3 tablespoons coarsely chopped oil-packed sun-dried tomatoes

1 small handful flat-leaf parsley

1 sprig oregano

¼ teaspoon smoked paprika

2 lemons, divided

¼ cup extra virgin olive oil

Kosher salt

Freshly ground black pepper

2 tablespoons butter, divided

1 lb halloumi

1 small bunch Tuscan kale, rapini, or Swiss chard

Fine herbs, such as chives, parsley, or basil, for garnish

Note:

If you don't have a food processor, blended sauces like romesco and pesto can be made using a stand, smoothie, or immersion blender. If using a stand blender, you will have to scrape down the sides a few times and may also need to add a little more oil to achieve a saucy consistency.

A tomato-and-pepper-based sauce originating in the Spanish region of Catalonia, romesco is my current fave no-cook sauce to add to everything from sandwiches and pasta to fish and chicken. The sauce is sometimes thickened with bread, but I prefer its texture without. When you pair it with pan-fried halloumi and sautéed greens, this super quick dish is a showstopping vegetarian main.

In a small pan, toast the almonds over medium heat until lightly browned and nutty smelling, 1 to 2 minutes. Transfer to the bowl of a food processor along with two of the garlic cloves, the roasted red peppers, sun-dried tomatoes, parsley, oregano, smoked paprika, and the juice and zest from one lemon. Pulse a few times to chop and mix. Add the oil and blend into a smooth sauce. Taste and season with salt and pepper, if needed, and set aside. This sauce can be made up to 1 week in advance and stored in the fridge.

Place a large nonstick skillet over medium heat and add 1 tablespoon of butter.

Slice the halloumi into twelve equal pieces and halve the remaining lemon. Sear the halloumi and lemon for 4 to 5 minutes, flipping the halloumi once, until golden brown. Remove to a plate and set aside.

Add the remaining 1 tablespoon of butter along with the kale, season with salt and pepper, and cook until lightly wilted, 1 to 2 minutes. Grate in the remaining garlic clove and cook for another minute.

Spread the sauce onto a platter or divide between four shallow dishes or plates. Top with the greens and seared halloumi, and squeeze the lemon juice overtop, to taste. Scatter the top with some fresh herbs and serve.

Curried Lentil Stuffed Squash

SERVES 4

2 acorn squashes, halved lengthwise

3 tablespoons olive oil, divided

2 tablespoons maple syrup

Kosher salt

Freshly ground black pepper

¾ cup brown lentils

3 cups low-sodium vegetable broth

1 medium red onion, finely diced

1 stalk celery, finely diced

1 green apple, finely diced

3 garlic cloves, finely grated

1 tablespoon curry powder

1 lemon, juiced

2 handfuls baby spinach

½ cup dried cranberries

½ cup dried apricots, finely diced

½ cup chopped walnuts

2 tablespoons finely chopped cilantro

2 tablespoons finely chopped parsley

3½–5 oz crumbled feta

Note:

If you have another variety of dried lentils, swap them in. Red lentils cook the fastest, taking about 20 minutes, and green lentils such as the fancy French Puy variety take 40 to 45 minutes. And if you're looking for instant lentils, just open a can.

When Aaron and I first started dating, he'd always pitch stuffed bell peppers as a dinner option. Since he was so committed to this idea, I didn't have the heart to tell him that I just don't really like cooked bell peppers enough to warrant eating a whole one for dinner, no matter how good the stuffing is. I can't fully explain how much this very strange and innocuous little thing fills my heart, but this stuffed squash is my olive branch to that pepper-obsessed twenty-something, offered about twelve years late.

Preheat your oven to 400°F and place the acorn squash halves in a baking dish, cut side up.

Drizzle the flesh with about 1 tablespoon of oil followed by the maple syrup. Season with salt and pepper and roast for 35 to 45 minutes, depending on the size of the squash, until fork tender.

Meanwhile, rinse the lentils in a fine-mesh sieve, inspecting for any bad lentils or debris. Transfer them to a saucepan and add the vegetable broth. Place the pot over high heat and bring to a boil. Cover the pot with a lid, reduce the heat to a low simmer, and cook for 20 to 25 minutes or until the lentils are tender but not mushy. Drain the lentils, transfer to a large bowl, and set aside.

While the lentils cook, heat 1 tablespoon of oil in a large skillet over medium heat. Add the onion, celery, and apple, season with salt and pepper, and cook for 5 to 7 minutes or until tender and lightly caramelized. Stir in the garlic and curry powder, cook for another 30 seconds to 1 minute, then stir in the lemon juice, scraping the bottom of the pan to pick up any burned-on bits. Stir in the spinach and transfer into the lentil bowl.

Add the cranberries, apricots, walnuts, cilantro, and parsley and mix well to combine.

Divide the mixture into the roasted acorn squash and scatter with the feta. Drizzle the top with the remaining tablespoon of oil and bake for 10 to 15 minutes or until the feta is golden brown.

BANG FOR
YOUR BUCK

FAST
FLAVOR

ONE
POT-ISH

Stewed White Beans with Greens & Chili

SERVES 4

2 slices stale bread

3 tablespoons olive oil, divided

3 teaspoons finely chopped rosemary, divided

½ teaspoon crushed red pepper flakes

Kosher salt

Freshly ground black pepper

1 shallot, thinly sliced

2 garlic cloves, thinly sliced

½–1 red finger chili, thinly sliced

2 cans (19 fl oz each) cannellini beans

1 cup low-sodium vegetable or chicken broth

2–3 cups chopped dark leafy greens

1 lemon, zested and juiced

¼ cup finely chopped parsley

2 tablespoons finely chopped oregano

3½ oz crumbled goat cheese

Note:

To save some cash, swap canned cannellini beans for 1 cup of dried. Cover with a few inches of water and leave on the counter to soak for 8 hours or up to 1 day. Drain, transfer to a pot, and cover with a few inches of fresh water. Bring to a boil, then reduce the heat to low and gently simmer for 2 hours or until tender, adding more water if needed. Drain and season with salt.

While they tend to get a bit of a bum rap due to certain schoolyard rhymes, I'll just come right out and say it: beans slap. Shelf-stable and full of protein, beans work with pretty much any savory flavor you pair them with and bring rich creaminess to any dish. They are delicious pureed or stirred into soups and chili, and even when acting as the main event, they hold their own.

Blitz the bread in a food processor or tear into small pieces to make rough breadcrumbs.

Heat 1 tablespoon of oil in a sauté pan over medium heat. Add the breadcrumbs along with 1 teaspoon of the chopped rosemary and the red pepper flakes. Season with salt and pepper and cook, stirring frequently, until golden and crisp, 3 to 5 minutes. Transfer the crumbs to a plate and set aside.

Add the remaining 2 tablespoons of oil to the pan along with the shallot. Season with salt and pepper and cook until softened and lightly golden brown, 2 to 3 minutes. Stir in the garlic, chili to taste, and remaining rosemary, and cook for another 1 to 2 minutes.

Drain and rinse the beans, then add them to the pan. Using the back of a spoon or a potato masher, lightly mash about one-third of the beans. Pour in the broth, bring the mixture to a simmer, and cook down until thickened and the liquid has reduced by about half. Stir in the greens and cook until tender, about 3 minutes for heartier greens and about 1 minute for more delicate greens.

Finish the beans with the lemon zest, lemon juice, parsley, and oregano, and season to taste with salt and pepper.

Serve in shallow bowls topped with the goat cheese and toasted breadcrumbs.

Quick Coconut Butter Tofu with Chickpeas

SERVES 4 TO 6

FAST
FLAVOR

GET
AHEAD

ONE
POT-ISH

2 tablespoons butter

2 yellow onions, diced

Kosher salt

Freshly ground black pepper

½–1 serrano or jalapeño chili
pepper, diced

¼ cup finely chopped cashews

3 garlic cloves, finely grated

3–4 tablespoons finely grated
ginger

1 teaspoon coriander seeds

1 tablespoon garam masala

1 teaspoon ground turmeric

1 teaspoon cumin

½ teaspoon ground cardamom

¼ teaspoon chili powder

1 can (5 oz) tomato paste

1 can (13 fl oz) coconut milk,
well shaken

1–2 tablespoons packed
brown sugar

¾–1 lb extra-firm tofu,
large dice

1 can (19 fl oz) chickpeas,
drained and rinsed

2 handfuls coarsely chopped
dark leafy greens

½ lemon, juiced

Cilantro, for serving

Tomato paste is one of my favorite "low and slow in a hurry" shortcuts. For things like tomato sauce, chili, and even in this butter tofu, tomato paste brings the rich, savory flavor of slow-cooked tomatoes, and all you need to do is open a can.

Heat the butter in a large saucepan over medium heat. Add the onions, season with salt and pepper, and cook for 5 to 7 minutes or until softened and lightly golden. Add the chili and cashews and cook for another 1 to 2 minutes or until the chili is soft.

Stir in the garlic, ginger, coriander seeds, garam masala, turmeric, cumin, cardamom, and chili powder. Cook for 30 seconds to take the edge off the garlic and ginger and to toast the spices. Add the tomato paste, stirring well to combine, and cook for 1 to 2 minutes. Carefully pour in ½ cup of water and scrape any stuck-on bits off the bottom of the pan.

Add the coconut milk and 1 tablespoon of brown sugar, lower the heat to medium-low, partially cover the pot with an off-kilter lid, and allow the sauce to simmer for 5 to 10 minutes to thicken slightly and allow the flavors to meld.

Using a stand blender or immersion blender, blitz the sauce until smooth. Return to the pan, season to taste with salt and another tablespoon of brown sugar, if needed, and stir through the tofu, chickpeas, and greens. Cover and cook until the tofu and chickpeas are heated through and the greens are wilted, about 5 minutes.

Stir in the lemon juice and serve over rice or with naan, scattered with cilantro.

Note:

This sauce stores and reheats beautifully so I suggest making a double batch. You can store it in the fridge for up to 5 days or in the freezer for up to 3 months. My favorite way to freeze sauces and stewy things is to transfer them to a large freezer bag, lay it flat on a small baking sheet, and freeze until solid. By freezing it flat, storage is super simple and it defrosts quickly.

Creamy Polenta with Greens, Tomatoes & Cheese

SERVES 4

1 batch Basic Polenta, recipe on page 248

1 can (27 fl oz) whole tomatoes

6 garlic cloves, divided

1 onion, cut into thin wedges

2 anchovy fillets, minced, optional

2 sprigs rosemary

2 tablespoons olive oil, divided

Kosher salt

Freshly ground black pepper

2 large handfuls leafy greens, such as chard, kale, or collards, coarsely chopped

½ teaspoon crushed red pepper flakes

½ teaspoon cumin

3½ oz soft or semi-soft cheese, such as Brie, Taleggio, or Raclette

2 tablespoons red pepper jelly

½ cup finely grated Parmigiano-Reggiano cheese

¼ cup finely chopped parsley

Note:

The sweet/spicy finish of the red pepper jelly really makes this dish. If you don't have red pepper jelly on hand, a drizzle of honey and some crushed red pepper flakes will do the trick.

Somewhere between pasta and mashed potatoes, polenta is the perfect bed for pretty much anything you want to spoon over it. This veg-heavy topping of roasted tomatoes, slightly crisp greens, oozy cheese, and red pepper jelly is my personal fave.

Preheat your oven to 400°F.

Prepare a batch of Basic Polenta and keep warm over low heat.

Meanwhile, add the tomatoes along with their juices into a 9-by-13-inch baking pan. Thinly slice four garlic cloves and add to the pan along with the onion, anchovies, rosemary, and 1 tablespoon of oil. Season with salt and pepper, stir to combine, and roast for 25 to 30 minutes or until the tomatoes have cooked down and the onion is soft.

In a bowl, toss together the greens, red pepper flakes, and cumin with the remaining tablespoon of oil and season with salt and pepper. Place the greens on top of the tomatoes and return to the oven for 8 to 10 minutes, until the greens are softened and starting to crisp around the edges.

Remove the vegetables from the oven, top with the soft cheese and dot with the red pepper jelly. Place the pan under a high broiler for 3 to 4 minutes or until the cheese is melted and golden brown.

Remove the lid from the polenta, whisk in the Parmigiano-Reggiano cheese and parsley, and season to taste with salt and pepper, if needed.

Serve the polenta in shallow bowls topped with the cheesy greens and tomatoes.

Mushroom Stroganoff

SERVES 4

8–10 oz cremini or white mushrooms, sliced or quartered

Kosher salt

Freshly ground black pepper

3 tablespoons butter, divided

1 yellow onion, finely diced

4 garlic cloves, finely grated

½ teaspoon dried thyme

2 tablespoons brandy

2 tablespoons all-purpose flour

2 cups vegetable or mushroom broth

2–3 teaspoons Worcestershire sauce

12 oz egg noodles

½ cup sour cream

¼ cup finely grated Parmigiano-Reggiano cheese

½ lemon, juiced

2 tablespoons chopped parsley

1–2 tablespoons chopped dill

For those nights I'm in a rush when I don't really want pasta but I don't _not_ want pasta, you know?

Place a large sauté pan over medium heat. Add the mushrooms to the dry, hot pan, season with salt and pepper, and cook, stirring frequently, until slightly cooked down and starting to color around the edges, about 3 minutes.

Add 1 tablespoon of butter along with the onion, season with salt and pepper, and continue to cook until the onion and mushrooms are golden, 3 to 5 minutes. Stir in the garlic and thyme and cook for 30 seconds to 1 minute. Deglaze the pan with the brandy and allow it to boil away completely. If using a gas stove, turn the heat off under the pan before adding the brandy to avoid accidental flare-ups. Remove the mushrooms and onions from the pan and set aside.

With the pan still on medium heat, add the remaining 2 tablespoons of butter to melt, then sprinkle the flour overtop. Stir well to combine and cook for 1 minute to toast the flour. Slowly stir in the broth and Worcestershire sauce, to taste, and bring the mixture to a simmer. Add the mushrooms and onions back in, turn the heat down to low, and allow the sauce to thicken.

Bring a large pot of salted water to a boil. Cook the egg noodles according to the package directions until al dente. Strain the noodles and divide among four shallow bowls or plates.

Finish the sauce with the sour cream, Parmigiano-Reggiano, lemon juice, parsley, and dill and serve over the noodles.

Note:

That _je ne sais quoi_ of Worcestershire sauce, which is made with fermented anchovies, is pretty difficult to replace, but there are a few good vegan varieties you can find online and in specialty stores for those who avoid eating fish

Pasta

Creamy Spaghetti al Limone

SERVES 4 TO 6

Kosher salt

1 lb spaghetti

4 large egg yolks

⅓ cup whipping cream

½ cup finely grated
Parmigiano-Reggiano
cheese, plus more for serving

1 lemon, zested and juiced

2 tablespoons finely chopped
parsley

Freshly ground black pepper

The first time I made spaghetti al limone was in university. As a lifelong lemon lover, I was hooked from the first bite. My roommate, Megan, however, had other feelings. After taking a big bite straight from the pot, encouraged by my raving, she grimaced. "That tastes like Skittles." For those like Megan, who may be a little more lemon-wary, this creamy version tames the sharp bite of lemon juice, leaving you with the most perfect velvety lemony bite.

Bring a large pot of salted water to a boil and cook the spaghetti until al dente or cooked to your liking.

Meanwhile, in a large bowl, whisk together the egg yolks and whipping cream. Add the grated Parmigiano-Reggiano, lemon zest, lemon juice, and parsley, and season with some salt and a good amount of freshly ground black pepper.

When the pasta is cooked, turn off the heat and scoop about 1 cup of the starchy cooking liquid out of the pot. Drain the rest of the pasta and return it to the pot. Immediately pour in the lemony egg and cream mixture and stir well to combine. Slowly add some of the hot starchy pasta water to the pasta just to loosen up the sauce, about 2 tablespoons at a time.

Plate the pasta and serve immediately topped with some more grated Parmigiano-Reggiano and freshly ground black pepper, if desired.

Note:

Like with spaghetti carbonara, the hot pasta will lightly cook the egg yolk, creating a creamy and thick sauce. If you are avoiding undercooked egg yolks, you can leave them out of this sauce. Just increase the cream to ½ cup and the cheese to 1 cup. You will need to stir quite vigorously and add additional starchy cooking liquid to reach a thick and creamy consistency.

Pantry Puttanesca

SERVES 4 TO 6

FAST
FLAVOR

ONE
POT-ISH

PANTRY
STAPLE

1 tablespoon olive oil

1 yellow onion, finely diced

Kosher salt

Freshly ground black pepper

2 garlic cloves, thinly sliced

4–6 anchovy fillets

3 tablespoons tomato paste

¼ cup dry white wine or vodka, optional

1 can (27 fl oz) crushed tomatoes

1 teaspoon crushed red pepper flakes

1 lb dried pasta, any shape

½ cup chopped kalamata olives

½ cup sliced roasted red peppers

½ cup sliced oil-packed sun-dried tomatoes

3 tablespoons capers

6 oz oil-packed tuna, drained

3 tablespoons finely chopped parsley, plus more for serving

1 tablespoon finely chopped oregano, plus more for serving

Note:

Oil-packed tuna is a real treat, especially the stuff you find in a jar, but a regular can of water-packed solid or chunk tuna would also be delish.

Puttanesca is a true pantry dish—the recipe was literally created to use up whatever you've got hanging around. Tomatoes and garlic form the base of the sauce while capers and olives provide a little brininess and red pepper flakes add spice. Additional ingredients like onion, booze, anchovies, sweet peppers, and tuna are all things that I have on hand but feel free to swap in any sweet, spicy, briny, or funky ingredients you think would work.

Place a large skillet or sauté pan over medium heat and add the oil. Add the onion, season with salt and pepper, and cook for 3 to 4 minutes or until softened and lightly golden brown. Stir in the garlic and anchovies and cook until the anchovies break down, about 1 minute. Stir in the tomato paste and cook for 1 to 2 minutes to bring the flavors together.

Deglaze the pan with the wine and cook down for about 1 minute to reduce the liquid by half. If you don't have any wine on hand or are avoiding alcohol, deglaze the pan with ¼ cup water. Carefully pour in the crushed tomatoes, stir in the red pepper flakes, and bring to a simmer. Turn the heat down to medium-low and cover the pan with an off-kilter lid to allow steam to escape.

While the sauce simmers, bring a large pot of water to a boil over high heat. Season well with salt and cook the pasta according to the package directions until al dente. Reserve about 1 cup of the cooking liquid, then drain the pasta and set aside.

Stir the olives, roasted red peppers, sun-dried tomatoes, and capers into the sauce and season to taste with more pepper. You should not need more salt as the anchovies, olives, and capers are all quite salty. Add the pasta, tuna, parsley, and oregano and stir well to combine. If the sauce is a little thick, add the reserved cooking liquid about ¼ cup at a time until the sauce has a silky consistency.

Serve immediately scattered with more oregano and parsley, if desired.

Caprese Baked Rigatoni alla Vodka

SERVES 4

1 lb rigatoni

Kosher salt

3 tablespoons butter

1 large shallot, finely minced

Freshly ground black pepper

3 garlic cloves, finely grated

1 cup cherry tomatoes, halved

1 can (5 oz) tomato paste

¼ cup vodka

½ cup whipping cream

½ cup finely grated
    Parmigiano-Reggiano cheese

1 ball burrata

1 cup grated mozzarella cheese

4–6 heaped tablespoons
    basil pesto

3 tablespoons coarsely
    chopped basil

Note:

Whenever a recipe calls for stove-to-oven preparation, I like to save on dishes and use a high-sided oven-safe sauté pan or large cast-iron skillet. Bonus points if it's nice enough to serve from!

Does a glug of vodka *really* add anything to a pot of already delicious tomato sauce? The simple answer is yes! Tomatoes contain certain flavors that are only brought out through the introduction of other ingredients. Some of these flavors require fat like butter, oil, or cream, some need a bit of water, and some just need a little splash of alcohol to really sing. With this rich and creamy vodka sauce, you're hitting all those notes.

Preheat your oven to 400°F.

Cook the pasta in boiling salted water according to package directions, just until al dente. Reserve 1 cup of pasta water and drain.

For the sauce, melt the butter in a large oven-safe sauté pan over medium heat. Add the shallot, season with salt and pepper, and cook until lightly golden brown, 2 to 3 minutes. Stir in the garlic and cook for 30 seconds before adding the tomatoes and tomato paste and seasoning with salt and pepper. Cook for 2 to 3 minutes to allow the cherry tomatoes to cook down and to further intensify the tomato flavor, then carefully deglaze the pan with the vodka. Let the vodka bubble away for 1 to 2 minutes to allow the alcohol to cook off, then turn the heat down to low and stir in the whipping cream and Parmigiano-Reggiano. Season to taste with salt and pepper.

Add the pasta as well as ½ cup of the reserved pasta water and stir to combine, adding more of the pasta water if needed to reach a saucy consistency. Gently tear the burrata open and set in the center of the pasta. Scatter the mozzarella around the edge to cover the rest of the pasta and dot the top with pesto.

Bake for 20 minutes or until the cheese is melted and golden brown. If desired, turn the broiler to high for the last minute of cooking for a deeper golden-brown color. Allow the pasta to cool for 5 minutes before serving, scattered with basil.

Miso Butter Corn Pasta

SERVES 4

FAST
FLAVOR

ONE
POT-ISH

PANTRY
STAPLE

FOR THE TOPPING

1 tablespoon butter

1 garlic clove, finely grated

¼ cup panko breadcrumbs

¼ teaspoon crushed red
  pepper flakes

Kosher salt

FOR THE PASTA

¾ lb orecchiette or other
  small pasta

¼ cup butter

2 shallots, finely minced

Kosher salt

Freshly ground black pepper

2 garlic cloves, finely grated

2 tablespoons white miso
  paste

1½ cups corn kernels, fresh,
  canned, or frozen and
  thawed

1 lemon, zested and juiced

½ cup finely chopped chives

I know it sounds mushy, but I really don't think I'd be able to do what I do without help from Aaron. He's my go-to taste tester, the world's best dish-doer, an A+ DJ who knows exactly what playlist to put on to match my mood, and, in the case of this recipe, a pretty great prep cook. At the end of a particularly long day, he offered to do the final test of this recipe while I sat with a cold glass of chardonnay coaching him through it. Needless to say, he crushed it.

Make the topping by heating a large sauté pan over medium heat. This pan will seem too big for this topping, but by using a large pan here, you can reuse it for the pasta, saving on dishes. Melt in the butter and add the garlic, breadcrumbs, and red pepper flakes. Cook, stirring frequently, for 1 minute until the panko is golden and toasted. Season with salt, transfer to a bowl, and set aside.

For the pasta, bring a large pot of water to a boil, season well with salt, and cook the orecchiette according to the package directions until al dente. Reserve 1 cup of the pasta cooking liquid before draining.

Meanwhile, place the sauté pan back over medium heat. Melt in the butter and add the shallots. Season with salt and pepper and cook for 5 to 6 minutes, or until the shallots are tender and lightly caramelized. Add the garlic, cook for 30 seconds, then stir in the miso paste. Add the corn and cook for 4 minutes just until tender.

Stir the lemon zest and juice into the corn mixture and add ½ cup of the pasta cooking liquid. To give the pasta a nice creaminess, use an immersion blender or small smoothie blender to blitz about half of the corn mixture until smooth. Return the blended sauce to the remaining corn mixture and add the cooked pasta.

continued

At this point, if the pasta and sauce are looking a little thick and claggy, stir in more of the pasta cooking liquid. Typically, I add at least another ¼ cup. Season to taste with salt and pepper, being a little reserved with the salt, as miso is quite salty.

Stir in the chives and serve with the crunchy topping.

Note:

As I watched Aaron make this recipe, I noticed for the first time that he stirs *a lot* when he's sautéing, and when I think about it, so do a lot of my friends and family who don't cook as often as I do. If this sounds like you, take it easy! When trying to build golden-brown color on anything from onions to breadcrumbs to meat, you need to let it sit in the pan a little unless a recipe specifically tells you to stir constantly. If you're worried about the food burning, just turn down the heat.

Mushroom & Pesto Skillet Lasagna

SERVES 6

GET
AHEAD

ONE
POT-ISH

SIMPLY
SNAZZY

¾ lb mushrooms, sliced

Kosher salt

Freshly ground black pepper

2 teaspoons olive oil

2 garlic cloves, finely grated

¼ cup dry white wine

4 large handfuls baby spinach

2 tablespoons butter

3 tablespoons all-purpose flour

2 cups warm milk

¾ teaspoon dried oregano

¼ teaspoon freshly grated nutmeg

2 cups ricotta cheese

⅓ cup prepared pesto

1 cup finely grated Parmigiano-Reggiano cheese, divided

1 cup grated mozzarella or fontina cheese, divided

1 egg

7 oz no-boil lasagna sheets

Since it's a casserole that goes from oven to table in the same pan, lasagna can give the appearance of being a low-dish, easy-breezy dinner. For those in the know, however, it typically is a full day-long production leaving piles and piles of dirty dishes in its wake. With this skillet lasagna, I've taken every shortcut I could think of and made a lasagna that is truly a one-pot wonder.

Preheat your oven to 375°F.

Place a dry 10-inch cast-iron or oven-safe skillet over medium heat. Add the mushrooms, season with salt and pepper, and cook for 5 to 7 minutes, until the mushrooms are golden brown.

Add the oil and garlic and continue to cook for 30 seconds. Deglaze the pan with the white wine and stir in the spinach to wilt for 30 seconds to 1 minute. Transfer the spinach and mushrooms to a bowl and set aside.

Return the pan to the heat to make the bechamel. Add the butter to melt and sprinkle the flour overtop. Whisk in and cook for 1 minute, until lightly golden brown, to toast the flour. While whisking, slowly add the warm milk. If any lumps form, just keep whisking. They will cook out. Season with ½ teaspoon of salt and stir in the oregano and nutmeg. Turn the heat down to medium-low and simmer for 5 minutes or until thickened. Transfer the bechamel to a bowl or spouted measuring cup and set aside. Turn the heat off under the pan and leave it on the stove.

In a bowl, combine the ricotta with the pesto and ½ cup each of the grated Parmigiano-Reggiano and mozzarella. Add the egg, season with ½ teaspoon of salt and pepper, and mix well to combine.

continued

Note:

If you are avoiding wine, or just don't want to open a bottle, you can use a little white wine vinegar whenever a small amount of white wine is called for in a recipe. Unless the wine is an integral ingredient, like in beef bourguignon, add about 1 tablespoon of vinegar in place of ¼ cup of wine.

Assemble the lasagna by spreading one-third of the bechamel across the bottom of the skillet. Lay one-third of the noodles in a single layer on top, breaking off pieces of the noodles as needed. Top with half of the ricotta mixture and scatter one-third of the mushrooms and spinach overtop. Repeat these layers. Top with the remaining noodles, spread the rest of the bechamel and mushroom mixture overtop, and scatter the remaining grated cheese over that. At this point, you can cover the pan and refrigerate for up to 24 hours before baking.

Spray the dull side of a piece of aluminum foil with nonstick cooking spray. Cover the lasagna, dull side down, and bake for 45 minutes. Carefully remove the foil and continue to bake for 15 to 20 minutes or until golden brown on top.

Allow the lasagna to sit for at least 10 minutes before slicing and serving.

Creamy Lobster Gnocchi

SERVES 3 TO 4

Kosher salt

1 lb prepared gnocchi

4 (about 3½ oz each) lobster
tails, fresh or frozen and
thawed

2 sprigs tarragon

⅔ cup 35% whipping cream

1 tablespoon butter

1 shallot, finely diced

Freshly ground black pepper

2 garlic cloves, finely grated

½ cup dry white wine

1 lemon

½ teaspoon crushed red
pepper flakes

3 tablespoons finely chopped
chives, plus more for serving

3 tablespoons coarsely
chopped tarragon, plus
more for serving

**Unless I'm making dinner at the seaside, cooking and breaking
down a whole lobster is a lot of messy work. Sticking with just
the tail makes it easy to prepare, and you get a better meat-to-
shell ratio. And hey, since you're paying for the shells too, this
creamy lobster gnocchi puts them and their hidden flavor to
good use.**

Bring a large pot of water to a boil over high heat. Season well with
salt and cook the gnocchi according to the package directions.
Reserve 1 cup of the cooking liquid, then drain the gnocchi and
set aside.

Remove the lobster meat from the shells by cutting down the length
of the rounded top with a pair of kitchen shears. Hold a lobster tail in
a folded kitchen towel and firmly squeeze the sides together until the
shell cracks. Pull the meat from the shells, cut into bite-sized pieces,
and set aside. Add the shells to a small saucepot along with the sprigs
of tarragon, and pour in the cream. Place over low heat and cook,
stirring and pressing the shells occasionally, while you prepare the
rest of the sauce.

Place a large sauté pan over medium heat. Add the butter and shallot,
season with salt and pepper, and cook for 3 to 4 minutes, until
softened and lightly golden. Stir in the garlic, then add the lobster
meat. Cook for 1 to 2 minutes, stirring frequently, until the lobster
meat is opaque and just cooked through. Remove the lobster meat
from the pan and set aside.

Add the wine to the pan, bring to a boil, and cook down until reduced
by half, about 2 minutes.

Remove the cream from the heat and, using a fine-mesh strainer,
strain the cream into the shallot mixture, leaving the shells and
tarragon sprigs behind. Zest in the lemon, add the red pepper flakes,
and turn the heat down to medium low. Simmer for 2 to 3 minutes to
reduce slightly.

continued

Add the gnocchi and cook until heated through and the sauce has thickened. The sauce will look a little loose at first, but the starch from the gnocchi will bulk it up. Stir in the lobster, add the juice of half of the lemon as well as the chopped chives and tarragon, and season to taste with salt, pepper, and more lemon juice, if needed. If the sauce is too thick, add a splash of the cooking liquid.

Serve immediately topped with more fresh herbs, if desired.

Note:

Whenever I'm splurging on a fancy ingredient like lobster or prime rib, the recipe had better be as simple as possible! Whether it comes together quickly like this gnocchi dish or involves very little actual input, if I'm splurging with my wallet, I need to be saving on time or effort.

Spicy Sausage Pasta
with Rapini & Herbed Ricotta

SERVES 4 TO 6

Kosher salt

¾–1 lb rapini

1 lb spaghetti or linguini

1 tablespoon olive oil

3 garlic cloves, thinly sliced

Freshly ground black pepper

5 oz sobrasada, nduja, or raw
   chorizo sausage (see note)

3 cups tomato passata or
   crushed tomatoes

2 tablespoons finely chopped
   parsley, divided

2 tablespoons finely chopped
   basil, divided

1 tablespoon finely chopped
   oregano, divided

½ cup ricotta

¼ cup finely grated
   Parmigiano-Reggiano
   cheese, plus more for serving

½ lemon, zested and juiced

Crushed red pepper flakes,
   optional

**Rapini, also known as broccoli rabe—which is arguably the
more fun name if you're a fan of *The Office*—is a bitter green
vegetable that looks like leafy, long broccoli. The bitterness
works well in this sauce to counteract the spice of the sausage,
but if bitter greens aren't your thing, you can substitute a
couple of handfuls of chopped kale or spinach stirred into
the sauce at the end just to wilt.**

Heavily season a large pot of water with salt and bring it to a boil over
high heat. Cook the rapini for 3 minutes or until bright green and
tender. Remove from the water with tongs, coarsely chop, and set
aside. Add the pasta to the boiling water and cook just until al dente.
Reserve about ½ cup of the cooking liquid before draining the pasta
and setting aside.

Meanwhile, set a large sauté pan over medium heat. Add the oil and
garlic, season with salt and pepper, and cook just until the garlic
softens, about 1 minute. Add the sausage and render for about
1 minute if using sobrasada or nduja, or 5 to 7 minutes or until
cooked through if using chorizo.

Turn the heat down to medium-low, stir in the passata, and allow the
sauce to reduce for about 3 minutes, stirring occasionally. Add the
pasta and a splash of the reserved cooking liquid and cook, tossing
often and adding more cooking liquid if needed, until the pasta is
cooked to your liking and the sauce has thickened, about 3 minutes.
Stir in the rapini and half of the parsley, basil, and oregano.

continued

In a small bowl, combine the ricotta, Parmigiano-Reggiano, lemon zest and juice, and the remaining herbs. Season to taste with salt and pepper and scatter with crushed red pepper flakes for some extra spice, if desired.

Serve the pasta topped with the ricotta and an extra scattering of Parmigiano-Reggiano.

Note:

Sausage is a great flavor shortcut. Someone has already taken the time to season it with salt, spices, and herbs, so all you have to do is add it to your recipe. In this recipe, spicy cured Spanish sobrasada (not to be confused with Italian soppressata) or fermented Italian nduja, available at specialty food stores, are soft, spreadable sausage varieties that almost melt into the sauce, giving it a deep, peppery flavor. If you can't find either, raw or uncured chorizo will work well.

Fish

Baked Fish Butty

SERVES 4

2 tablespoons butter

½ cup panko breadcrumbs

½ cup (about 12) finely crushed saltine crackers

½ teaspoon garlic powder

Kosher salt

Freshly ground black pepper

1 egg

2 tablespoons mayonnaise

1 teaspoon Dijon mustard

1 lb cod loin, about 2 small loins

FOR SERVING

¼ cup mayonnaise

½ lemon, zested and juiced

2 tablespoons finely chopped dill pickle or pickle relish

1 tablespoon capers, chopped

2 teaspoons finely chopped parsley

Kosher salt

Freshly ground black pepper

4 soft burger buns

4 slices processed cheese

Pickle slices or coins

There is a particular fast-food sandwich that I have an unreasonable amount of love for. It's a sleeper hit on the menu, and when I take that first bite, I am in flavor heaven. As amazing as it is, I do have one bone to pick with it: why only half a slice of processed cheese? It feels strangely stingy. But rather than pick a fight with a clown, a big purple monster, and a very specific burglar, I'll just make my own.

Preheat your oven to 425°F and lightly grease a baking sheet with nonstick cooking spray or line it with parchment paper.

Melt the butter in a large skillet over medium heat and add the breadcrumbs, crushed crackers, and garlic powder. Season with ½ teaspoon of salt and a pinch of pepper, and toast, stirring frequently, until golden brown, about 2 minutes. Transfer the crumbs to a shallow dish and allow to cool to room temperature.

Meanwhile, in a separate shallow dish, whisk together the egg, mayonnaise, and mustard.

Cut the cod into four equal pieces about the size of your buns and, using paper towel, dry off the outside of each piece. Dip the cod into the egg mixture, then press into the toasted crumbs to coat and transfer to the prepared baking sheet, leaving a few inches of space between each piece.

Bake for 14 to 16 minutes or until the center flakes. To test, I like to stick a butter knife in the middle of one of the fillets and twist. If the fillet flakes, it's ready.

Stir together the mayonnaise, lemon zest, lemon juice, chopped pickle, capers, and parsley for a quick tartar sauce. Season to taste with salt and pepper. If desired, toast the buns. Spread the top bun with the tartar sauce and lay a piece of cheese on the bottom bun. Top with the crispy fish and a few pickle slices and serve.

Note:

The loin of a fish is the thickest part of the fillet that runs along the upper back. If you can't find cod loins at your grocery store or fish market, simply trim the thinner belly section off the bottom of the fillet, saving this thinner piece in the fridge or freezer to cook later. I like to fry it in oil until crisp, flake it with a fork, and add it to my Pantry Puttanesca (recipe on page 97) in place of the tuna.

Note:

In a lot of my recipes, I suggest coarsely chopping or even mincing ingredients before adding them into a food processor. But that seems counterintuitive, right? Why would I mince or chop something that's going into a machine to be chopped? Well, it has to do with friction. The longer you have to process something, the more friction the ingredients experience, and thereby, heat. By chopping delicate ingredients like herbs or fish, it reduces the amount of processing time and heat exposure, keeping flavors fresh.

Sesame Shrimpies

SERVES 4

GET
AHEAD

SIMPLY
SNAZZY

1 lb raw shrimp, shells and tails removed, divided

3 green onions, finely chopped

2 garlic cloves, finely grated

1 tablespoon finely grated ginger

½ teaspoon kosher salt

¼ teaspoon freshly ground black pepper

3 teaspoons toasted sesame oil, divided

2 teaspoons cornstarch

½ teaspoon fish sauce, optional

½ teaspoon sugar

1 egg white

1 tablespoon canola oil

2 tablespoons sesame seeds

4 burger buns

Mayonnaise

Grainy Dijon mustard

Hoisin sauce

Sriracha sauce

Lettuce or alfalfa sprouts

When my brother and I were little and my mom would have friends over for a fancy shindig, there was one rule: don't go near the shrimp ring until thirty minutes after everyone has arrived. Like a thief in the night, I can polish off a shrimp ring faster than you can say "oooh, a shrimp ring!" For a shrimp monster like me, these fresh and gingery shrimp burgers are my absolute dream.

Add half of the shrimp to the bowl of a food processor along with the green onions, garlic, ginger, salt, and pepper. Process until quite smooth and well combined. Transfer the mixture to a large bowl and set aside.

Dice the remaining shrimp and add to the bowl along with 2 teaspoons of sesame oil, the cornstarch, fish sauce, and sugar and mix well to evenly combine. In a separate bowl, whisk the egg white until frothy, then mix into the shrimp. Cover and set aside in the fridge for 20 to 30 minutes. This mixture can be made up to 1 day in advance if stored in the fridge in a sealed container.

Heat a large nonstick skillet over medium-high heat. Add the remaining teaspoon of sesame oil as well as the canola oil to the skillet. Divide the shrimp mixture into four portions and spoon it directly into the pan to form four patties. This method has more in common with making pancakes than shaping and frying traditional burgers, but I find it both easier and tidier. Scatter the uncooked top of each burger with sesame seeds.

Cook the burgers for 3 to 4 minutes per side or until golden and cooked through. Allow the burgers to rest for 5 minutes while you prepare the buns and toppings.

Toast or grill the buns and spread one side with mayo and mustard, and the other with hoisin and sriracha. Top with lettuce or alfalfa sprouts and a shrimp burger and serve immediately.

Crispy Coconut Fish Tacos

SERVES 4

GET
AHEAD

SIMPLY
SNAZZY

FOR THE SLAW

½ small cabbage

½ small red onion

½ jalapeño

½ cup diced fresh pineapple

1 avocado, diced

¼ cup chopped cilantro

½ teaspoon cumin

1 teaspoon sugar

1 lime, juiced

2 tablespoons extra virgin olive oil

1–2 tablespoons apple cider vinegar

Kosher salt

Freshly ground black pepper

FOR THE CHIPOTLE CREAM

¾ cup sour cream

2 teaspoons pureed or finely chopped chipotle peppers in adobo sauce (see note on page 12)

1 lime, zested and juiced

Kosher salt

FOR THE FISH

2 haddock fillets

1 egg

2 tablespoons mayonnaise

1 teaspoon chipotle peppers in adobo sauce

1 cup panko breadcrumbs

½ cup shredded unsweetened coconut

Kosher salt

3–4 tablespoons canola oil

For years, whenever my buddy Kyle would come over for dinner, he'd request my deep-fried fish tacos. While I do still bust that recipe out on special occasions, there's really no denying how messy and involved deep-frying at home can be. As a switch-up to the classic deep-fried version, these coconut-crusted pan-fried fish tacos are quick and easy to make, and trust me, you won't miss the deep fry.

For the slaw, thinly slice the cabbage, onion, and jalapeño and add to a large bowl along with the pineapple, avocado, and cilantro. Add the cumin, sugar, lime juice, oil, and 1 tablespoon of vinegar and season with salt and pepper. Taste and add more vinegar, salt, or pepper if needed and set aside. If you are making the slaw more than 1 hour in advance, keep it in the fridge. It will keep for up to 3 days.

For the chipotle cream, whisk together the sour cream, chipotles, lime zest, and lime juice and season to taste with salt. Set aside in the fridge until ready to use.

Prepare the fish by cutting the haddock into roughly 1-by-3-inch pieces. In a shallow dish, beat together the egg, mayonnaise, and chipotles until smooth. In a second shallow dish, combine the breadcrumbs and coconut and season with salt.

Working with one piece of fish at a time, dunk it into the egg mixture to evenly coat and allow any excess to drip off. Transfer the fish to the breadcrumb mixture and turn to coat. Set the breaded piece aside onto a plate and continue until all the fish is coated.

Place a large sauté pan or skillet over medium-high heat and add enough of the oil just to coat the bottom of the pan. When hot, fry the fish for 2 to 3 minutes per side or until golden brown and cooked through. If necessary, cook in batches

continued

8–12 corn or flour tortillas

Cilantro

Lime wedges

Meanwhile, heat the tortillas according to the package directions or directly over a gas burner until warm and lightly charred.

Serve the crispy coconut fish on warm tortillas topped with slaw, chipotle cream, a scattering of cilantro, and a wedge of lime.

Note:

If you'd prefer to bake the fish, pre-toast the panko in about 1 tablespoon of canola oil over medium heat for 2 to 3 minutes. Set aside to cool, then mix with the coconut, season with salt, and coat the fish as directed. Once coated, the fish can be baked at 425°F for 8 to 10 minutes or until crisp and cooked through. You can also freeze the coated fish for up to 3 months and cook from frozen at 425°F for 15 to 17 minutes.

Smoked Fish Brandade

SERVES 4 TO 5

GET
AHEAD

SIMPLY
SNAZZY

1 lb russet potatoes

Kosher salt

¾ cup 18% table or
35% whipping cream

1 sprig woody herb, such as
rosemary, thyme, or sage

5 garlic cloves, divided

½ lemon, zested and juiced

⅛ teaspoon cayenne pepper

⅛ teaspoon smoked paprika

Freshly ground black pepper

5 oz hot-smoked fish, such as
mackerel or salmon

2 tablespoons finely chopped
parsley

4 tablespoons olive oil

5 tablespoons finely grated
Parmigiano-Reggiano
cheese

Sliced sourdough or baguette,
for serving

I first had *brandade de morue* at one of my and Aaron's favorite Toronto restaurants, Le Sélect Bistro. It is the setting of many impromptu after-work dates and was where we signed a legal contract about being in love forever (a.k.a. where we got married). To bring our cherished date spot home, I've simplified the classic. Brandade is traditionally made with salt cod, but I've swapped that time-consuming ingredient for hot-smoked fish, giving this version an amazing smoky flavor. If you need any more convincing, it's a potato dish that you serve with bread. What could be better than that?

Preheat your oven to 400°F and grease a 9-inch casserole dish or baking pan with nonstick cooking spray, oil, or butter.

Peel the potatoes and cut into large chunks. Add to a large pot and cover with cold tap water. Season well with salt and bring to a boil over high heat. Cook the potatoes until fork tender, 15 to 20 minutes. Drain the potatoes, transfer back into the pot, cover, and set aside.

Meanwhile, add the cream and herb sprig to a small saucepan. Grate in four garlic cloves and place over medium heat. Bring the cream to a simmer, turn the heat down to low, and cook for 10 minutes to mellow the garlic and bring the flavors together.

Strain the cream through a fine-mesh sieve into the potatoes. Add the lemon zest, lemon juice, cayenne, and paprika. Season with salt and pepper and, using a hand mixer, blitz until smooth and creamy.

Finely shred the fish, add to the potatoes along with the parsley and oil, and blitz to combine. Season to taste with salt and pepper. Transfer the mixture to the prepared casserole dish or baking pan. At this point, you can cover the dish and refrigerate it for up to 1 day.

Scatter the top with the Parmigiano-Reggiano and bake for 20 minutes until golden brown and bubbling.

continued

Meanwhile, toast the bread. Cut the remaining garlic clove in half and rub the cut side of the garlic onto the hot toast.

Serve the brandade and toast as an appetizer or serve with a salad or blanched greens as a main.

Note:

In addition to using salt cod, brandade is traditionally whipped into an ultra-smooth puree in a food processor. But rather than risk the gluey potato mess that can come with over-processing potatoes and overdeveloping their starch, I like to stick with a hand mixer.

Lemony Shrimp with White Beans & Garlic Toast

SERVES 4

FAST
FLAVOR

ONE
POT-ISH

PANTRY
STAPLE

2 tablespoons butter, divided

1 lb raw shrimp, peeled

Kosher salt

Freshly ground black pepper

2 shallots, minced

4 garlic cloves, divided

1 tablespoon all-purpose flour

½ cup dry white wine

1 cup chicken or vegetable broth

¼ cup whipping cream

2 teaspoons Dijon mustard

1 teaspoon crushed red pepper flakes

½ teaspoon dried Italian seasoning

2 cans (18 fl oz each) white kidney beans, drained and rinsed

2 cups chopped kale

4 thick slices sourdough bread

½ cup finely grated pecorino cheese

1 lemon, zested and juiced

2 tablespoons finely chopped parsley

Pantry staples don't begin and end with my cupboards. There are a few things I always keep on hand in my fridge like feta, greens, and lemons, and my freezer is always stocked with a box or two of puff or phyllo pastry, a few bags of frozen fruit, and, of course, my favorite quick-cooking protein, frozen shrimp.

Melt 1 tablespoon of butter in a large sauté pan over medium-high heat. Dry off the shrimp with a piece of paper towel, season with salt and pepper, and sauté until cooked through and lightly golden, 1 to 2 minutes per side. Remove the shrimp to a plate and set aside.

Turn the heat down to medium and add the remaining tablespoon of butter along with the shallots. Season with salt and pepper and cook until softened and lightly golden brown, 4 to 5 minutes. Mince three of the garlic cloves, add to the shallots, and cook for another 30 seconds.

Stir in the flour and continue to cook for 30 seconds to 1 minute. Add the wine followed by the broth and cream. Stir in the mustard, red pepper flakes, and Italian seasoning and bring to a simmer. Allow the sauce to thicken for about 5 minutes, stir in the beans and kale, and turn the heat down to low.

Toast the bread in a toaster or under a high broiler until golden and crisp. Cut the remaining garlic clove in half, rub the cut side onto the hot toast, and set aside.

Stir the shrimp, pecorino, lemon zest, lemon juice, and parsley into the saucy bean mixture and serve alongside the garlic toast.

Note:

Shrimp have a simple tell to let you know when they're done. Uncooked shrimp hold a loose U shape, perfectly cooked shrimp form a C, and, O no, if your shrimp look like little O's, you've overcooked them.

Seared Carrot Ginger Salmon

SERVES 4

1 medium carrot, peeled and
finely grated

1 green onion, finely chopped

3 tablespoons finely grated
ginger

1 garlic clove, finely grated

½ cup rice wine vinegar

¼ cup soy sauce

2 teaspoons honey

¼ cup sesame oil

½ cup + 2 teaspoons canola
oil, divided

4 salmon fillets, about 5 oz
each

1–2 romaine hearts

½ cucumber, thinly sliced

1 cup cherry tomatoes, halved

**Even though I love cooking, I take every opportunity I can to
find shortcuts in the kitchen. From using food processors for
prep to taking grocery store shortcuts, I really do believe there
are no wrong moves if it's going to get you to enjoy making
food for yourself, your friends, and your family. In this recipe,
one sauce does twice the work. Half acts as a marinade for
fresh salmon fillets while the rest is used to dress a crisp and
crunchy salad reminiscent of a takeout sushi side.**

In a bowl or large jar, combine the carrot, green onion, ginger, garlic,
and vinegar. Add the soy sauce, honey, sesame oil, and ½ cup of the
canola oil and whisk or shake well to emulsify.

Pour half of the dressing into a shallow dish or freezer bag and add
the salmon, tossing to coat and arranging flesh side down, if using a
shallow dish. Cover and place in the fridge, along with the remaining
dressing, for at least 20 minutes or up to 1 hour.

Place a large nonstick skillet over medium-high heat. Remove the
salmon from the marinade and pat dry with paper towel. Add the
remaining 2 teaspoons of canola oil to the pan and sear the salmon,
flesh side down, until golden, 3 to 4 minutes. Flip and continue to
cook for 2 to 3 minutes or until cooked to your liking. Set aside to rest
while you prepare the salad.

Tear or chop the romaine and add it to a large bowl along with the
cucumber and tomatoes. Dress to your liking with the remaining
dressing and serve alongside the seared salmon.

Note:

Delicate proteins like fish marinate super quickly, especially
when an acid like vinegar or citrus is involved, so keep it to
1 hour or less. If you want to get ahead, you can marinate the
fresh fish, then remove from the marinade, dry off the outside,
cover, and store in the fridge for up to 1 day.

Lemony Piccata

SERVES 4

4 white fish fillets, such as
  tilapia, sole, or pickerel

Kosher salt

Freshly ground black pepper

½ cup all-purpose flour

2 tablespoons cornstarch

Olive oil

5 tablespoons cold butter,
  cubed and divided

1 shallot, minced

2 garlic cloves, finely grated

¼ cup dry white wine

2 lemons

3 tablespoons capers

3 tablespoons chopped
  parsley

With a sauce of butter, garlic, wine, lemon, and capers, piccata blends all my favorite rich, citrusy, briny flavors into one dish. As a pescatarian, I prefer my piccata with fish for obvious reasons, but you can substitute boneless, skinless chicken thighs for a great addition to your chicken repertoire.

Preheat your oven to 200°F.

Place a large skillet over medium-high heat. Using a piece of paper towel, dry off the fish fillets. Season both sides with salt and pepper.

In a shallow dish, combine the flour and cornstarch and season with a pinch of salt and pepper. Lightly dredge the fish in the flour mixture, flipping to evenly coat, and tap off any excess.

Add 1 tablespoon of oil into the pan and fry the fish for 2 to 3 minutes per side until golden brown and cooked through. To avoid overcrowding the pan, fry the fish in batches, adding a splash more oil between each. Once fried, set the fish aside on a rack-lined baking sheet and transfer to the oven to keep warm.

Turn the heat down to medium and add 1 tablespoon of butter along with the shallot. Season with salt and pepper and cook for 3 to 4 minutes until softened and lightly golden brown. Stir in the garlic and cook for 30 seconds.

Deglaze the pan with the wine and bring to a simmer for 2 minutes to slightly reduce. Zest in one of the lemons, then add the juice of both. Whisk in the remaining butter, a small piece at a time, and continue whisking until a smooth sauce forms.

Stir in the capers and parsley and season to taste with salt and pepper. Transfer the fish to plates and spoon over the sauce.

Note:

Dredging protein in flour before searing or pan-frying helps add body and creaminess to pan sauces and stews. As some of the flour falls off the protein, it's left behind in the pan, which then helps thicken any liquid you add later on.

Tomato Trout

SERVES 4

Olive oil

¼ cup sliced sun-dried
tomatoes

1 tablespoon tarragon or basil,
plus more for serving

2 tablespoons butter, room
temperature

Kosher salt

Freshly ground black pepper

2 rainbow trout fillets

8 oz cherry tomatoes on
the vine

1 lemon, quartered

This is truly the fastest company-worthy dinner I've ever made. The full fillets of rainbow trout cook in a flash while the savory, almost molasses-y sweetness of sun-dried tomatoes provide intense flavor that makes the dish taste as if you tried harder than you actually did. By roasting cherry tomatoes on the vine alongside the trout, you end up with the perfect side or salad topper for a total "host with the most" vibe.

Preheat your oven to 425°F and drizzle a baking sheet with oil.

Finely mince the sun-dried tomatoes and tarragon and add to the butter. Season with salt and pepper and mash together to combine. Dry off the fish with paper towel and place the fillets skin side down onto the prepared baking sheet. Spread the tomato butter over the trout fillets.

Add the cherry tomatoes on the vine to the pan as well as the lemon quarters, cut side down, and drizzle with a little oil. Season with salt and pepper.

Roast for 15 to 17 minutes or until the trout is flaky and cooked through and the tomatoes are tender and beginning to burst.

To serve, use a fish spatula to lift the trout from the skin, and scatter with fresh tarragon, if desired, and a squidge of roasted lemon juice.

Note:

Roasting or grilling lemons is my favorite way to ensure I get as much juice from them as possible. The heat from the oven or grill makes the juices flow, giving you access to every drop of lemony goodness.

Note:

Like most salmon dishes, this is equally delicious when served cold. Prepare as directed and store the salmon and pickle separately in the fridge for up to 3 days.

Mediterranean Salmon

SERVES 6

GET
AHEAD

SIMPLY
SNAZZY

FOR THE SALMON

1½ lb salmon fillet, skin on

½ cup dry white wine

¼ cup + 1 tablespoon olive oil, divided

1 lemon, zested

3 garlic cloves, smashed and coarsely chopped

1 small handful dill

1 sprig oregano

1 sprig rosemary

¾ teaspoon kosher salt

½ teaspoon freshly ground black pepper

FOR THE FETA PICKLE

¼–½ red onion, thinly sliced

1 garlic clove, finely grated

Kosher salt

Freshly ground black pepper

1 lemon, juiced

2 tablespoons white wine vinegar

1 teaspoon honey

1 cup cherry tomatoes

½ English cucumber

3½ oz feta

½ cup pitted kalamata olives

¼ cup capers

3–4 tablespoons extra virgin olive oil

1 tablespoon finely chopped dill

2 teaspoons finely chopped parsley

1 teaspoon finely chopped oregano

In my house, salmon is the new chicken. Quick enough for a weeknight meal, yet snazzy enough to serve as a lighter version of a Sunday roast, I'm always looking for new ways to prepare it. In this recipe, a quick zesty marinade adds a ton of flavor to the salmon itself, and I don't know about you, but if I see the words "feta" and "pickle" together, I'm sold.

Place the salmon into a shallow baking dish or zip-top bag. Pour in the wine and ¼ cup of oil and add the lemon zest and garlic. Hold the dill, oregano, and rosemary in your hands and clap or lightly rub them until they smell fragrant. Add them to the salmon along with the salt and pepper and flip and toss to combine. Arrange the fish flesh side down and place in the fridge to marinate for 15 minutes to 1 hour.

Meanwhile, make the pickle by adding the onion and garlic to a large bowl and seasoning with a pinch of salt and pepper. (If you're a person who loves onion as much as I do, feel free to use the larger amount.) Pour in the lemon juice, vinegar, and honey and toss to combine. Set aside for 5 to 10 minutes to allow the garlic and onion to lightly pickle while you prepare the rest of the vegetables and feta.

Halve the tomatoes, dice or thinly slice the cucumber, and cut the feta into roughly ½-inch cubes. Add to the bowl along with the olives, capers, and extra virgin olive oil and pepper to taste. Toss to combine, then set aside while you cook the salmon.

Preheat your oven to 400°F.

Remove the salmon from the marinade and dry the fillet off with a few pieces of paper towel. Drizzle the salmon with the remaining tablespoon of olive oil and place onto a baking sheet or in a large baking dish. Season with salt and pepper and roast for 15 to 18 minutes or until the fish flakes easily when a fork is inserted into the center of the fillet and twisted.

Set your broiler to high and broil for 1 to 2 minutes or until the salmon is lightly golden. Transfer whole to a serving dish or slice and plate.

Finish the pickle mixture with the chopped dill, parsley, and oregano and spoon over the salmon.

Chicken

Satay Chicken Wings with Peanut Sauce

SERVES 4 TO 6

2 lb split chicken wings

½ cup coconut milk

3 tablespoons soy sauce

1 tablespoon fish sauce

3 garlic cloves

1 shallot, coarsely chopped

1 small handful cilantro stems,
  coarsely chopped, plus more
  for serving

2-inch piece ginger, minced

1 stalk lemongrass, thinly sliced

½–1 red Thai chili or
  ½ teaspoon cayenne pepper

2 teaspoons honey

2 teaspoons turmeric

Canola oil, for grilling

Chopped peanuts, for serving

FOR THE DIPPING SAUCE

½ cup natural peanut butter

¼ cup coconut milk

2 teaspoons fish sauce

1 lime, juiced

1 garlic clove, finely grated

2–3 tablespoons soy sauce

2–3 teaspoons hot chili sauce,
  like sriracha

Note:

These wings can also be
roasted in a 400°F oven on
a baking sheet lined with a
wire rack for 35 to 40 minutes
or until crisp and cooked
through. If roasting in the
oven, make sure there is some
room between each wing for
maximum crispiness.

These marinated and grilled wings are inspired by the flavors of Southeast Asian satay, a takeout favorite in my house. Satay is the national dish of Indonesia, made of seasoned, skewered, and grilled meat, typically served with a rich and flavorful peanut sauce. While nothing will compare to those little dunky skewers we order in, these wings (and the quick and fresh mango salad they're paired with) are the perfect play on a party staple.

Place the chicken wings in a large bowl or a heavy-duty freezer bag and set aside.

In a blender or food processor, combine the coconut milk, soy sauce, fish sauce, garlic, shallot, cilantro stems, ginger, lemongrass, Thai chili to taste, honey, and turmeric, and blitz until smooth. Pour the sauce over the chicken wings, tossing to coat, cover the bowl or seal the bag, and transfer to the fridge to marinate for at least 1 hour or up to overnight.

When ready to cook, preheat your grill to medium.

Remove the chicken wings from the marinade and, using a piece of paper towel, wipe as much of the marinade off as possible. Dip a piece of paper towel or cheesecloth in a little oil and, while holding it in a long pair of tongs, quickly oil the grill. Place the chicken wings onto the grill, allowing the wings to touch. This will create a little bit of steam while they cook, creating moisture to keep the wings juicy during their relatively long cook time.

Grill the wings for 25 to 30 minutes, flipping every 5 minutes or so, until cooked through and lightly charred. Set aside to rest for 5 minutes.

Make the peanut dipping sauce by whisking the peanut butter, coconut milk, fish sauce, lime juice, garlic, and soy sauce and chili sauce to taste.

Serve the chicken wings scattered with chopped peanuts and cilantro alongside the peanut dipping sauce and mango salad (recipe on next page), if desired.

continued

Mango Salad

2 limes, juiced

2 tablespoons fish sauce

2 teaspoons packed brown
sugar

½–1 red Thai chili, thinly sliced,
optional

1 shallot, thinly sliced

2 firm mangoes

1 red bell pepper

½ cup picked cilantro leaves

¼ cup chopped roasted
peanuts

In a large bowl, stir together the lime juice, fish sauce, brown sugar, chili, and shallot and set aside. Peel and slice the mangoes into ¼-inch sticks and add to the bowl. Thinly slice the bell pepper and add it along with the cilantro and peanuts to the bowl. Toss well to combine.

The salad will keep in the fridge for up to 2 days.

Chipotle Chicken Soup

SERVES 6 TO 8

FAST
FLAVOR

GET
AHEAD

ONE
POT-ISH

1 tablespoon olive oil

1 red onion, diced

Kosher salt

Freshly ground black pepper

1 small handful cilantro stems, leaves reserved

2 ears corn, kernels removed

3 garlic cloves, finely grated

1½ teaspoons cumin

1½ teaspoons chili powder

1 teaspoon smoked paprika

2 boneless, skinless chicken breasts

1 can (27 oz) crushed tomatoes

1 can (18 fl oz) black beans

¼ cup pureed or finely chopped chipotle peppers in adobo sauce

3½ cups low-sodium chicken broth

2 handfuls leafy greens, such as spinach, kale, or collards

½ cup sour cream

1 lime, halved

1 avocado, diced

2 radishes, thinly sliced

2 green onions, thinly sliced

Other than pie, soup is my mom's favorite food group. Growing up, there was a particular brand she loved that, in my opinion, was exorbitantly priced. We're talking over $10 in the early aughts for maybe two servings of soup. I've always been a fan of saving a buck, so with our stash of old mason jars ever growing, I took to making batches of soup on weekends to take my mom through the week. Some were more extravagant long-cooking recipes, while others, like this, could be thrown together in a flash.

Place a large pot over medium heat. Add the oil and onion, season with salt and pepper, and cook for 4 to 5 minutes until tender and lightly golden brown. Finely chop the cilantro stems, reserving the leaves for serving, and add to the pan along with the corn kernels, garlic, cumin, chili powder, and paprika. Cook for 1 to 2 minutes to lightly cook the garlic and corn and toast the spices.

Add the chicken breasts to the pot and pour in the tomatoes, black beans, chipotles, and chicken broth. Stir to combine and bring to a boil. Reduce the heat to a simmer, cover the pot, and cook for 15 to 20 minutes until the chicken is cooked through.

Remove the chicken from the soup and set it aside to rest for 5 minutes. Meanwhile, season the soup with more salt and pepper, if needed, stir in the greens, and keep the soup warm over low heat.

Using two forks, shred the chicken into bite-sized pieces and return to the soup. Serve the soup topped with a dollop of sour cream and a bit of lime juice, some avocado and radish, and a scattering of cilantro and green onions.

Cool any leftovers to room temperature before storing in containers or mason jars in the fridge for up to 3 days.

Note:

When making any type of chicken soup, I like to cook the chicken by poaching it in the broth. This infuses both the soup base and the chicken itself with even more chicken-y flavor.

Sheet Pan Souvlaki

SERVES 4 TO 6

GET
AHEAD

SIMPLY
SNAZZY

4 boneless, skinless chicken
   breasts

1 red onion, cut into thin
   wedges

4 tablespoons olive oil, divided

2 lemons, divided

4 garlic cloves, chopped

1 tablespoon dried oregano

1 teaspoon dried thyme

1 teaspoon smoked paprika

½ teaspoon crushed red
   pepper flakes

Kosher salt

Freshly ground black pepper

4 medium yellow potatoes

½ cup kalamata olives, pitted

½ cup sun-dried tomatoes,
   coarsely chopped

3½ oz feta

1 tablespoon finely chopped
   parsley

2 teaspoons finely chopped
   oregano

Tzatziki, store-bought or
   homemade, recipe follows

While some see brunch as the perfect catch-up meal between pals, my group of girlfriends understands that there is no better cuisine to vent and vehemently hand-talk over than Greek food. With sharing platters of souvlaki and potatoes, arguably too much feta, a boatload of dips, and a bottle of cheap white wine with ice and soda on the side for table-made spritzers, this downsized at-home version has the added benefit of not requiring hard pants.

Cut each chicken breast into five equal chunks. I like to cut off the pointed end, then cut the rest of the chicken breast in quarters. Place the chicken in a large bowl or shallow baking dish along with the onion. Add 3 tablespoons of the oil along with the zest and juice of one lemon, garlic, oregano, thyme, paprika, and red pepper flakes. Season with ½ teaspoon of salt and ¼ teaspoon of black pepper and mix well to combine. Cover and place in the fridge to marinate for at least 30 minutes or up to overnight. Cut the remaining lemon into quarters and set aside.

Meanwhile, cut the potatoes into large chunks and place in a pot of cold water. Season well with salt and bring to a boil. Cook the potatoes just until fork tender, about 10 minutes. Drain the potatoes and set aside to steam dry in the strainer.

Set your oven rack to the lowest position, place a large baking sheet onto the rack, and preheat the oven to 450°F. Once at temperature, add the remaining tablespoon of oil to the sheet pan and carefully transfer on the potatoes. Season with salt and pepper and roast for 15 to 20 minutes or until the undersides are golden.

Meanwhile, retrieve the chicken from the fridge and thread the pieces onto four bamboo skewers. Remove the pan from the oven, flip the potatoes, add on the chicken skewers and quartered lemon, and pour over any remaining marinade. Carefully toss to combine and return to the oven to roast for 15 minutes or until the chicken is cooked through.

continued

Gently stir in the olives and sun-dried tomatoes and scatter the feta overtop. Turn on the broiler to high and cook for 3 to 5 minutes or until the feta is lightly golden and the chicken has a bit of charring on it.

Allow the pan to rest for 5 to 10 minutes, then top with parsley and oregano and serve with the tzatziki.

Note:

This parboil/hot pan potato technique is my go-to method for guaranteed crispy potatoes. By parboiling the potatoes, the inside steams while the outside gets extra starchy, leading to the crispiest exterior and fluffiest interior ever.

Tzatziki

½ English cucumber, halved lengthwise and seeds removed

Kosher salt

1 lemon, zested and juiced

2 garlic cloves, finely grated

1½ cups plain Greek yogurt

2 tablespoons extra virgin olive oil

3 tablespoons finely chopped dill

1 tablespoon finely chopped mint, optional

1 tablespoon finely chopped parsley, optional

Freshly ground black pepper

Cut the cucumber in half lengthwise and, using a spoon, scrape out most of the seeds. If desired, remove the peel. Grate the cucumber on the large side of a box grater and transfer to a fine-mesh sieve. Sprinkle 1 teaspoon of salt over the cucumber and toss well to combine. Place the sieve in a sink or over a bowl and allow it to sit for at least 15 minutes or up to 1 hour to drain away some of the water. This will concentrate the cucumber flavor and help keep your tzatziki thick.

In a large bowl, combine the lemon zest, lemon juice, and garlic. Stir to combine and set aside for 30 seconds to 1 minute to allow the lemon juice to take the raw edge off the garlic. Add the yogurt, oil, dill, and mint and parsley if desired, and mix well to combine.

Give the cucumber a firm press or squeeze with either your hands or a clean kitchen towel to remove as much water as possible, then add it to the yogurt and mix well. Season with pepper and more salt, if needed, and place in the fridge until ready to use.

Chick Parm Meatballs

SERVES 4

GET
AHEAD

ONE
POT-ISH

SIMPLY
SNAZZY

Olive oil

1 yellow onion, finely minced

Kosher salt

Freshly ground black pepper

3 garlic cloves, divided

⅓ cup fine breadcrumbs

¼ cup milk

1 lb ground chicken

1 egg

1½ cups finely grated
    Parmigiano-Reggiano
    cheese, divided

4 tablespoons finely chopped
    parsley, divided

4 tablespoons finely chopped
    basil, divided

3 teaspoons finely chopped
    oregano, divided

7 oz cocktail bocconcini,
    divided

1 cup cherry tomatoes, halved

¼ cup dry white wine or water

1 can (27 fl oz) crushed
    tomatoes

I'm always looking for new ways to reinvent Aaron's favorite meals. With these chicken Parmesan meatballs, I'm bringing his two most requested dinners together into one cheesy meal perfect for spooning over pasta, serving on a bun, or just eating straight from the pan.

Preheat your oven to 375°F.

Set a large cast-iron or nonstick skillet over medium heat and add 1 tablespoon of oil. Add the onion, season with salt and pepper, and cook for 3 to 4 minutes until tender and lightly golden brown. Grate in one garlic clove, cook for an additional 30 seconds, then remove the onion mixture to a large bowl and set aside to cool completely.

In a small bowl, stir together the breadcrumbs and milk and set aside to allow the breadcrumbs to hydrate, about 10 minutes.

Add the chicken to the cooled onion mixture along with the egg, the breadcrumb mixture, 1 cup of the grated Parmigiano-Reggiano, 2 tablespoons each of the parsley and basil, and 1½ teaspoons of the oregano. Season with ¾ teaspoon of salt and some black pepper.

Using your fingers almost like rakes, gently and thoroughly mix everything together, being careful not to squeeze the mixture in your hands, as that would lead to tough meatballs.

Place twelve bocconcini onto a work surface and set the rest aside. Divide the meatball mixture into twelve equal pieces and flatten each one into a circle. Place one ball of bocconcini into the center of each circle and fold the meatball mixture around the cheese, pinching to seal. At this point, you can transfer the meatballs to a plate, cover, and store in the fridge for up to 1 day.

Turn the heat under the pan on to medium-high and add 2 teaspoons of oil. Working in batches if needed, sear the meatballs until golden brown but not yet fully cooked, flipping once, 1 to 2 minutes per side, then set aside on a plate.

continued

Note:

If you're looking for a retro chicken parm vibe with extra-stretchy cheese, substitute the fresh bocconcini with classic brick pizza mozzarella. Cut 2½ oz into twelve ½-inch cubes to stuff into the meatballs and grate 3½ oz for scattering overtop.

Add 1 teaspoon of oil to the pan along with the cherry tomatoes and grate in the remaining two garlic cloves. Season with salt and pepper and cook for 30 seconds to 1 minute or until the tomatoes start to cook down. Deglaze the pan with the wine, scraping any burned-on bits off the bottom of the pan, then add the crushed tomatoes. Stir in the remaining basil, parsley, and oregano.

Nestle in the meatballs and scatter the remaining bocconcini and ½ cup of Parmigiano-Reggiano overtop. Transfer to the oven and bake for 15 to 18 minutes or until the meatballs are cooked through. Turn on the broiler to high and cook for 2 minutes or until golden brown.

Allow the meatballs to rest for 5 to 10 minutes, then serve as-is or with your favorite pasta, with crusty bread for dunking, or on a bun as a deliciously sloppy sandwich.

Roasted Garlic Bread Chicken Thighs

SERVES 4

FAST
FLAVOR

PANTRY
STAPLE

8 boneless chicken thighs,
skinless or skin on

¼ cup butter, room temperature

2 teaspoons finely chopped
parsley

1 teaspoon finely chopped sage

1 teaspoon finely chopped
rosemary

1 tablespoon + ¼ cup ground
Parmesan cheese, divided

8 garlic cloves, unpeeled,
divided

Kosher salt

Freshly ground black pepper

4 slices country or sourdough
bread, ¾ inch thick

½ teaspoon garlic powder

1 tablespoon olive oil

2 shallots, cut into wedges

1 sprig sage

2 sprigs rosemary

Note:

There is a flavor compound
in garlic called allicin that is
produced when cloves are
chopped, sliced, crushed, or
minced. By mincing garlic,
you are intensifying the flavor
and allowing it to spread
more thoroughly throughout
a recipe. By roasting it whole,
especially in its skin, you
end up with little nuggets of
mellow, sweet garlic flavor. In
this recipe, you get the best
of both worlds.

I'm not even going to beat around the bush: while real Parmigiano-Reggiano cheese is delicious, I find it tends to burn more quickly, so just go full "ground Parmesan" and use the cheap stuff. The nutty funkiness of shaky cheese brings out the flavors of the garlic, and it makes a perfect golden crust on the chicken.

Preheat your oven to 375°F and set the chicken on the counter while the oven comes to temperature.

In a small bowl, stir together the butter, parsley, sage, rosemary, and 1 tablespoon of the Parmesan cheese. Peel and finely mince two cloves of garlic, stir into the butter mixture, and season with salt and pepper. Spread the garlic butter over both sides of each piece of bread and place in a row on a baking sheet.

Season the chicken with salt and pepper. In a small bowl, stir together the remaining ¼ cup of Parmesan cheese with the garlic powder and sprinkle over the chicken. Flip and press the chicken to evenly coat in a thin layer of the cheese mixture.

Heat the oil in a large sauté pan or skillet over medium-high heat and sear the chicken skin side down for 2 minutes or until lightly golden brown. You'll need to do this in two batches. Transfer the chicken, seared side up, onto the garlic bread. Arrange so that each piece of bread has two thighs on top.

Add the shallots and remaining unpeeled garlic cloves to the pan along with the sprigs of sage and rosemary and cook until slightly softened, 2 to 3 minutes. Scatter over the chicken and transfer to the oven.

Roast for 20 to 25 minutes or until the internal temperature of the chicken reaches 165°F.

Loosely tent the pan with aluminum foil and allow it to rest for 5 to 10 minutes before serving.

FOOD
WASTE

ONE
POT-ISH

SIMPLY
SNAZZY

BLT Chicken

SERVES 4

½ cup sun-dried tomatoes
   in oil

2 garlic cloves

½ cup fresh basil

¼ cup finely grated
   Parmigiano-Reggiano
   cheese

2 tablespoons toasted
   pine nuts

Kosher salt

Freshly ground black pepper

4 slices stale whole wheat
   bread

1½ oz bacon or pancetta,
   coarsely chopped

2 tablespoons olive oil

¼ cup all-purpose flour

2 eggs

¼ cup mayonnaise

4 boneless, skinless chicken
   breasts

1 handful arugula

Note:

To make stale bread for
breadcrumbs, bread
pudding, stuffing, or French
toast, spread the slices into
an even layer and leave on
the counter for a few hours
or up to overnight.

**Whenever I'm looking for ways to freshen up chicken breasts,
I look to the classics. By adding bacon or pancetta to the
breadcrumbs and stuffing the breasts with a quick sun-dried
tomato pesto of sorts and spicy arugula, you get all the flavors
of a classic BLT in every bite.**

Preheat your oven to 425°F and line a baking sheet with parchment
paper or aluminum foil, dull side up.

In the bowl of a food processor, blitz together the sun-dried tomatoes
and garlic to coarsely chop them. Add the basil, Parmigiano-Reggiano,
and pine nuts and pulse a few times to combine. Add 2 tablespoons of
the oil from the sun-dried tomatoes and season with salt and pepper.
Process to your desired consistency, adding up to 2 more tablespoons
of the sun-dried tomato oil if you like. Transfer the pesto to a dish
and set aside.

Roughly tear up the bread and add it to the food processor along
with the bacon. Pulse to combine and finely chop into small crumbs.
Add the oil, season with salt and pepper, and blitz.

Turn the breadcrumbs out into a shallow dish. Scatter the flour into
a second shallow dish and season with salt and pepper. In a third,
beat together the eggs and mayonnaise. Set aside.

Prepare the chicken for stuffing by cutting a slit in the side. To do
this, place a breast onto a stable work surface and place your palm
on top. Using a sharp knife, hold it parallel to the board and carefully
cut a pocket about three-quarters of the way through. Using a spoon,
divide the pesto evenly among the chicken breasts and stuff each
with some arugula.

Dredge the chicken in the flour, tapping off as much excess as
possible, followed by the egg mixture. Press into the breadcrumbs
and transfer to the prepared baking sheet.

Roast the chicken for 25 to 30 minutes or until golden brown and the
internal temperature of the meat reaches 165°F. Allow the chicken
to rest for 5 minutes before serving.

Fresh & Grilled Ratatouille with Provençal Chicken

SERVES 4

FOR THE CHICKEN

4 chicken legs

¼ cup olive oil

½ cup dry white wine

4 garlic cloves, coarsely chopped

1 lemon, zested

1 tablespoon herbes de Provence

4 sprigs oregano

1 teaspoon kosher salt

½ teaspoon freshly ground black pepper

FOR THE RATATOUILLE

1 small red onion

2 tablespoons sherry vinegar

2 zucchinis

2 Japanese eggplants or 1 small Italian eggplant

1 medium field tomato, preferably heirloom

1 bell pepper

1 pint cherry tomatoes

1 lemon, juiced

3–4 tablespoons extra virgin olive oil

¼ cup parsley leaves

¼ cup basil leaves

1 tablespoon oregano leaves

4½ oz soft goat cheese

Chicken legs, sometimes sold as chicken leg quarters, are one of my favorite cuts to cook on the grill. Composed of the thigh, drumstick, and sometimes part of the back, this reasonably priced cut holds onto a ton of flavor and moisture even over the dry heat of a grill. This is the perfect meal for a French-inspired summer cookout, but napkins are a must as these bone-in morsels require some handheld dining.

Place the chicken legs in a large bowl or heavy-duty zip-top bag and pour in the oil and wine. Add the garlic, lemon zest, herbes de Provence, and oregano sprigs and season with the salt and pepper. Cover the bowl or seal the bag and transfer to the fridge to marinate for at least 30 minutes or up to 12 hours.

Remove the chicken from the marinade, pat it dry with paper towel, and set aside on a plate on the counter for 30 minutes to take off the chill of the fridge. Meanwhile, heat your grill to medium.

Season the chicken with salt and pepper and place on the grill, skin side up. Close the lid and cook for 30 to 35 minutes or until deeply golden and crisp around the edges and the internal temperature reaches 165°F.

While the chicken grills, prepare the ratatouille. Trim and peel the whole onion and slice about three-quarters of it into ¼-inch disks. Thinly slice the remaining onion and add it to a large bowl with the vinegar to pickle. Thinly slice the zucchinis and eggplants and cut the field tomato into wedges.

When cooked, remove the chicken from the grill and set it aside to rest for at least 10 minutes while you grill the vegetables.

continued

Turn the heat on the grill up to high. Add the slices of onion and the whole bell pepper onto the grill along with the eggplant and half of the zucchini. Toss the cherry tomatoes onto a piece of aluminum foil and place on the grill. Cook the vegetables until tender and charred, about 4 minutes for the zucchini, eggplant, and tomatoes and about 6 minutes for the onion and bell pepper.

Set the bell pepper aside in a small bowl, cover with a plate or a piece of plastic wrap, and let it steam for a few minutes to loosen the charred skin. Peel off as much of the charred skin as possible and thinly slice the pepper into strips. Add the grilled and raw vegetables to the bowl with the pickled onion. Add the lemon juice, oil, and parsley, basil, and oregano and season with salt and pepper.

Scatter the goat cheese overtop and serve alongside the grilled chicken.

Note:

The chicken can also be roasted in a 400°F oven for 40 to 45 minutes or until the internal temperature reaches 165°F. For the grilled veg, heat a large cast-iron skillet over medium-high heat and add a splash of oil. Cut the bell pepper, onion, zucchinis, and eggplants into large chunks and cook along with the cherry tomatoes until charred. You won't get the same grilled flavor or effect, but the contrast between the cooked and raw vegetables will still be delicious.

Chicken Noodle Roast Chicken

SERVES 4 TO 6

1 whole chicken

2 tablespoons butter,
room temperature

1 teaspoon turmeric

1 teaspoon chicken bouillon

Kosher salt

Freshly ground black pepper

2 leeks, cut into 1-inch pieces
(see note)

2–3 field carrots, peeled and
cut into 1-inch pieces

2 stalks celery, cut into 1-inch
pieces

½ fennel bulb, thinly sliced
and fronds reserved

2 garlic cloves, thinly sliced

3 sprigs fresh thyme

1¼ cups orzo or pearl couscous

¼ cup dry white wine, optional

4 cups low-sodium chicken
broth

1 tablespoon chopped parsley

If you can't tell by now, I am really into recipe mash-ups. I'll blame it on my general and lifelong inability to decide what I want to cook and eat. With its bright-yellow color from the turmeric, this roast brings together a company-worthy classic and my childhood fave, neon-yellow chicken noodle soup from a packet.

Preheat your oven to 450°F.

Spatchcock or flatten the chicken by removing the backbone. To do this, flip the chicken over so that it sits breast side down and, using a pair of kitchen shears, carefully cut along either side of the backbone. Flip the bird over and press down to flatten it.

In a bowl, mash together the butter, turmeric, and bouillon. Using your fingers or a small spoon, separate the skin from the chicken breasts and thighs and spread half of the butter mixture as evenly as possible under the skin.

Place a braiser or heavy-bottomed roasting pan over medium-high heat. Season the chicken skin with salt and pepper, add half of the remaining butter mixture into the hot pan, and sear the chicken, breast side down, until golden, 5 to 8 minutes. Remove from the pan and set aside, breast side up.

Add the remaining butter to the pan along with the leeks, carrots, celery, and fennel and season with salt and pepper. Cook until the vegetables begin to pick up a little color, 6 to 8 minutes, stirring frequently. Stir in garlic, thyme sprigs, and orzo, and cook for 1 to 2 minutes.

Deglaze the pan with the white wine or ¼ cup of water, then add the chicken broth. Place the seared chicken, breast side up, into the pan and carefully transfer to the oven. If the pan looks a little full, place a large sheet pan or a piece of aluminum foil on the rack below in case of any boil-over. Cook for 40 to 45 minutes or until the internal temperature of the chicken reaches 165°F.

continued

If the chicken skin begins to brown too much, place a lid or a piece of aluminum foil overtop.

When cooked through, remove from the oven and set aside to rest for 10 minutes. Scatter over the parsley and fennel fronds and serve.

Note:

To prepare and clean leeks, trim off the roots and dark-green tops. Chop the white and light-green parts and place in a large bowl filled with tap water. Run your hands through the leeks, so that any dirt falls to the bottom of the bowl. Using your hands, scoop the leeks out of the water, allowing as much water as possible to drain away. If your leeks are particularly sandy, repeat this process with fresh water.

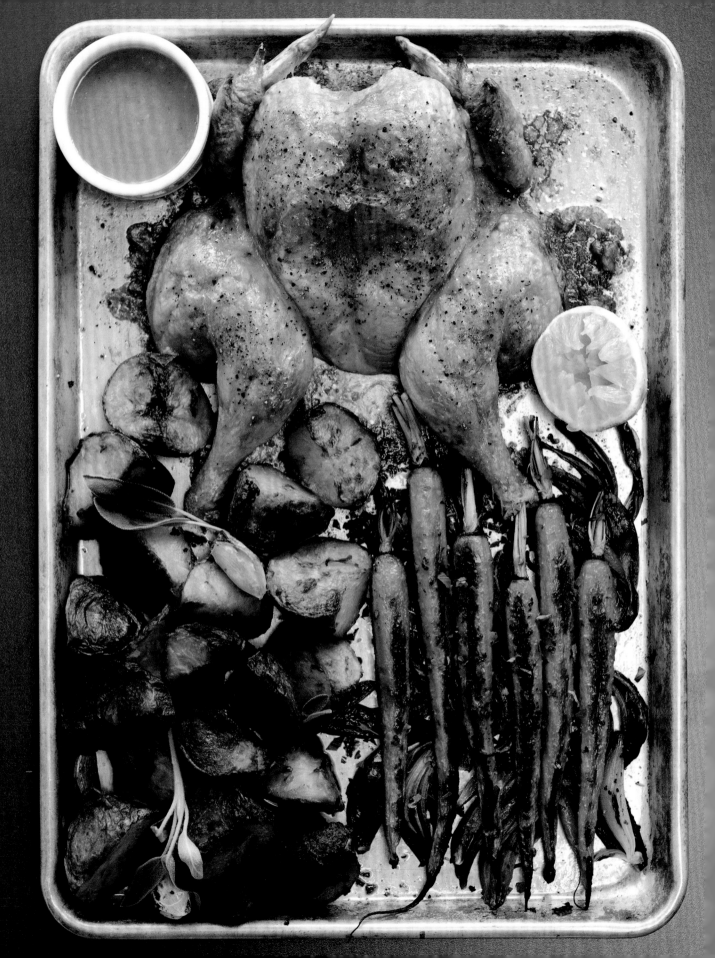

Sheet Pan Sunday Roast

SERVES 4

ONE POT-ISH

SIMPLY SNAZZY

1 whole chicken (3½ lb)

2 lb yellow potatoes, quartered

1 teaspoon baking soda

Kosher salt

4 tablespoons olive oil, divided

Freshly ground black pepper

4 sprigs sage, divided

4 garlic cloves, skins on

8 field carrots

2 small red onions, cut into 6 wedges

2 teaspoons grainy Dijon mustard

1 lemon

2 tablespoons chopped parsley

FOR THE GRAVY

2 tablespoons butter

2 tablespoons all-purpose flour

¼ cup dry white wine, optional

2–2½ cups low-sodium chicken broth

This sheet pan dinner is really just a reason to get quick homemade gravy into your life as often as you'd like, because it's a Sunday roast that's simple enough for any night of the week. If your classic roast dinner contains greens, add some sprouts or broccoli spears to the pan for the last 25 minutes of roasting.

Preheat your oven to 450°F and set out a large sheet pan or roasting pan. You'll want to use a pan that is big enough to fit the chicken and veg in a single layer.

Spatchcock or flatten the chicken by removing the backbone. To do this, flip the chicken over so that it sits breast side down and, using a pair of kitchen shears, carefully cut along either side of the backbone. Flip the bird over and press down to flatten it. Set aside at room temperature while you prepare the potatoes.

Place the potatoes in a large pot and cover with cold water. Stir in the baking soda, season heavily with salt, and bring to a boil over high heat. Boil the potatoes just until fork tender, 8 to 10 minutes, then drain and allow to air dry in the strainer for about 5 minutes.

Drizzle both sides of the chicken with 1 tablespoon of the olive oil and season well with salt and pepper. Place the chicken on one side of the pan, nestling two sprigs of sage underneath. Add the potatoes back into the pot or into a large bowl along with the whole garlic cloves and remaining sprigs of sage. Gently toss with another tablespoon of oil and a pinch of salt to fluff up the outside of the potatoes and develop some starchy coating.

Coat the other half of the pan with 1 tablespoon of oil and add the potatoes, garlic, and sage. Spread into an even layer and roast the potatoes and chicken for 20 minutes.

Meanwhile, slice any large carrots in half lengthwise. Toss the carrots and onions with the mustard and 1 tablespoon of oil and season with salt and pepper. Remove the pan from the oven, flip the potatoes, and add the carrots and onions to the pan.

continued

This recipe sort of uses a seafood boil approach to cooking—that is, adding ingredients based on the time it takes for them to cook. By parboiling the potatoes and staggering the addition of vegetables, you are able to cook all of the components for the appropriate time without having to worry about juggling different pots and pans.

Return to the oven, reduce the heat to 400°F, and continue roasting for 30 to 35 minutes or until the vegetables are golden brown and tender and the internal temperature of the chicken reaches 165°F.

Remove the chicken to a cutting board, loosely tent with aluminum foil, and set aside to rest for at least 10 minutes. Transfer the potatoes and garlic to a serving dish and zest half of the lemon overtop. Zest and juice the remaining half of the lemon over the carrots and onions and scatter with the parsley. Transfer to a serving dish and cover the veg to keep warm while you make the gravy.

For the gravy, place the sheet pan over medium heat and melt in the butter. Sprinkle the flour overtop and whisk well, making sure to scrape the bottom of the roasting pan to pick up any caramelized bits. Cook for 30 seconds to 1 minute to toast the flour, then, while whisking, slowly add the wine and 2 cups of chicken broth. Bring to a simmer and cook for 5 to 10 minutes or until the gravy reaches your desired consistency, adding another ½ cup of broth if needed. Serve alongside the chicken and veg.

Beef, Pork & Lamb

Pizza Today/Pizza Tomorrow

SERVES 3 TO 4

FAST FLAVOR

GET AHEAD

SIMPLY SNAZZY

FOR PIZZA TODAY

1 batch No-Yeast Flatbread, recipe on page 247

Olive oil

FOR PIZZA TOMORROW

2 cups bread flour

1 tablespoon skim milk powder, optional

1½ teaspoons instant yeast

1½ teaspoons sugar

¾ teaspoon kosher salt

½–¾ cup warm water

1½ tablespoons olive oil

TOPPINGS

½ small red onion, thinly sliced

1 cup red grapes, halved

1–2 sprigs rosemary, leaves removed

2 garlic cloves, thinly sliced

1 tablespoon balsamic vinegar

3 tablespoons olive oil, divided

Kosher salt

Freshly ground black pepper

1 Italian sausage, spicy or mild

3½ oz goat cheese, crumbled

3 tablespoons chopped walnuts

Honey, for serving

I'm not typically one to do the whole "back in my day" thing but do you remember having to actually talk to a human person on the phone to order a pizza? Or having to call a number to know what time movies were playing?! I'm dating myself here, but my point is, ordering pizza is *literally* the easiest thing in the world now, so trying to convince you to make pizza at home can be a tall order. But with this recipe and its options for a quick no-yeast or a slow-rise crust, making pizza today or even pizza tomorrow can be *almost* as easy as getting delivery.

If making pizza today, set your oven rack to the lowest position and preheat it to 500°F. Prepare a batch of No-Yeast Flatbread and set aside to rest for 20 minutes. Using a rolling pin, roll it out on a lightly floured work surface into a 12- or 14-inch circle, transfer to a lightly oiled baking sheet and prepare the toppings.

If making pizza tomorrow or within the next 3 days, in a large bowl, stir together the flour, skim milk powder, instant yeast, sugar, and salt. Make a well in the center and add ½ cup of warm water and the oil. Stir into a shaggy dough, adding another ¼ cup of water if needed, then turn out onto a lightly floured work surface and knead for 3 to 4 minutes or until soft, smooth, and springy, adding more flour as needed. Transfer the dough into an oiled bowl, cover, and place in the fridge to rise overnight or for up to 3 days.

When ready to bake, remove the dough from the fridge and set aside at room temperature. Adjust your oven rack to the lowest position and preheat it to 500°F. Roll the dough out on a lightly floured work surface into a 12- or 14-inch circle, transfer to a lightly oiled baking sheet, and prepare your toppings.

For the toppings, place the onion, grapes, rosemary leaves, and garlic in a bowl. Pour in the balsamic vinegar and 2 tablespoons of the oil and season well with salt and pepper. Toss to combine, and then set aside.

continued

Place a small skillet over medium-high heat. Using your fingers, pinch off bite-sized pieces of sausage meat from the casing and add to the pan. Cook, stirring occasionally, until golden and cooked through, 3 to 4 minutes.

Scatter the grape mixture evenly over the dough, leaving about a 1-inch crust. Scatter the sausage overtop, and dot with the goat cheese and the walnuts. Drizzle with the remaining tablespoon of oil and season with salt and pepper.

Bake the pizza on the bottom rack of your oven for 14 to 16 minutes or until the crust is crisp and golden and the toppings are tender.

Drizzle the pizza with honey, slice, and serve immediately.

Note:

Perhaps you've been told that salt kills yeast but in small quantities that's not true. What salt does is slow the development of yeast and controls the rate of yeast fermentation, causing it to rise more gradually and giving the dough better texture and a more complex flavor. In addition to better flavor, it strengthens gluten, increases golden-brown color, and adds a necessary brightness to your dough.

Creamy Harissa Lamb Meatballs

SERVES 4 TO 6

2 tablespoons olive oil, divided

2 shallots, finely diced, divided

Kosher salt

Freshly ground black pepper

2 garlic cloves, finely grated

2 teaspoons minced ginger

1½ teaspoons cumin

1 teaspoon coriander

¼ teaspoon cinnamon

⅓ cup fine breadcrumbs

½ cup dry white wine, divided

1 lb ground lamb

¼ cup pine nuts or finely chopped walnuts, toasted

3 tablespoons finely chopped parsley, divided

2 tablespoons finely chopped mint, divided

4 teaspoons finely chopped oregano, divided

1 egg

1 can (5 fl oz) tomato paste

2–3 tablespoons harissa paste

½ cup full-fat plain Greek yogurt (see note)

½ lemon, zested and juiced

3½ oz crumbled feta cheese

4 cups cooked long-grain rice, for serving

Lamb is my mom's favorite protein. We don't have it often, as a leg of lamb takes a long time to roast, and a rack of lamb just feels a little too fancy for family dinner, but with these meatballs, a delicious lamb dinner is in reach any day of the week. If lamb isn't your thing, substitute ground turkey, chicken, or pork.

Place a large cast-iron skillet or deep sauté pan over medium heat and add 1 tablespoon of the oil. Add half of the shallots, season with salt and pepper, and cook for 3 to 4 minutes until tender and lightly golden brown. Add the garlic, ginger, cumin, coriander, and cinnamon, cook for an additional 30 seconds, and then remove the pan from the heat, transfer the shallot mixture to a large bowl, and set aside to cool completely.

In a small bowl, combine the breadcrumbs with ¼ cup of the white wine and set aside to allow the breadcrumbs to hydrate, about 10 minutes.

When the shallot mixture is cool, add the ground lamb and breadcrumb mixture as well as the pine nuts, 2 tablespoons of the parsley, 1 tablespoon of the mint, 2 teaspoons of the oregano, and the egg. Season with ¾ teaspoon of salt and ¼ teaspoon of pepper.

Using two forks or your fingers almost like rakes, gently and thoroughly mix everything together. Try not to squeeze the mixture together as you mix, or it will result in tough meatballs. Divide the mixture into roughly twenty walnut-sized mounds and roll into meatballs. If the mixture sticks to your hands, lightly dampen them with tap water before continuing to form the meatballs.

Turn the heat under the pan to medium-high and add the remaining tablespoon of oil. Sear the meatballs, in batches if needed, until golden brown but not yet fully cooked, flipping once, 1 to 2 minutes per side. Once browned, set them aside.

continued

Add the remaining shallots to the pan, season with salt and pepper, and cook for 3 to 4 minutes or until lightly caramelized. Stir in the tomato paste and cook for another 2 minutes to intensify the flavor. Deglaze the pan with the remaining ¼ cup of white wine and then stir in the harissa to taste and 1 cup of water.

Nestle in the meatballs, cover the pan with a tight-fitting lid, and bring to a simmer. Turn the heat down to medium-low and simmer for 10 to 15 minutes or until the meatballs are cooked through to 160°F.

Remove the lid and turn off the heat. Spoon a few tablespoons of the hot sauce into the yogurt and whisk to combine. Add the lemon zest and juice, stir in the remaining parsley, mint, and oregano, and swirl into the meatballs.

Scatter with feta cheese and serve over prepared rice.

Note:

If you heat yogurt too quickly, the protein in it can coagulate, giving your sauce a curdled texture. By tempering the yogurt with a little bit of the hot sauce, as you would with eggs and hot milk when making custard, you can slowly bring up the temperature of the yogurt, minimizing the chance of curdling. Also, be sure to use full-fat yogurt, as the fat helps protect the delicate proteins.

Roasted Sausage Sheet Pan Dinner

SERVES 4 TO 6

2 sweet potatoes, cut into wedges

1 large red onion, cut into wedges

3 tablespoons olive oil, divided

Kosher salt

Freshly ground black pepper

½ savoy cabbage or ¼ green or purple cabbage

1 bell pepper, thickly sliced

1 green apple, cored and cut into large wedges

6 garlic cloves, unpeeled

3 sprigs fresh sage

4–6 bratwurst or Italian sausages

¼ cup mayonnaise

¼ cup sour cream

1 tablespoon grainy Dijon mustard

½ lemon, juiced

This speedy low-dish dinner is in honor of the slowest cook I know: my buddy Kyle. He's a bit of a troubadour, and has been known to walk away from the stove mid-cooking to tell a tale, pour a drink, or flip a record, never to return. By bringing the elements of his favorite dinner together on one pan, this is hopefully a no-fail way for him to get dinner on the table in a timely manner.

Preheat your oven to 450°F.

Toss the sweet potatoes and red onion with 1½ tablespoons of the oil on a large baking sheet. Season with salt and pepper and roast for 20 minutes.

Meanwhile, prepare the cabbage. If using a savoy, cut it into four wedges. If using a denser green or purple cabbage, thinly slice it. Add the cabbage, bell pepper, apple, garlic cloves, and sage to a large bowl. Drizzle in the remaining oil, season with salt and pepper, and gently toss to combine. Remove the potatoes and onion from the oven, give them a flip, and add the vegetables in a single layer. Toss the sausages in the bowl with any remaining oil to coat, then nestle them on top. Return to the oven and roast for another 20 to 25 minutes or until the sausages are golden brown and cooked through and the vegetables are caramelized and tender.

Set the pan aside to allow the sausages to rest for about 5 minutes.

While the sausages rest, remove two of the garlic cloves from the vegetable mixture and squeeze the roasted garlic into a small bowl. Mash well with a spoon, then stir in the mayonnaise, sour cream, mustard, and lemon juice. Season with salt and pepper.

Serve the sausages and vegetables with the roasted garlic sauce on the side.

Note:

Don't splurge on your baking sheets. Pick some up at your local restaurant supply store instead. They are inexpensive, super sturdy, stackable, and they clean up like a dream.

Brine & Bake Pork Chops

SERVES 4

GET
AHEAD

PANTRY
STAPLES

SIMPLY
SNAZZY

FOR THE BRINE

¼ cup kosher salt

¼ cup packed brown sugar

2 teaspoons peppercorns

2 garlic cloves, coarsely
   chopped

1 cup cold lager

4 pork chops, 1 inch thick

FOR THE COATING

2 tablespoons butter

¾ cup panko breadcrumbs

½ teaspoon garlic powder

½ teaspoon dried thyme

½ teaspoon celery salt or
   kosher salt

¼ teaspoon smoked paprika

¼ teaspoon cayenne pepper

¼ teaspoon onion powder

¼ cup ground Parmigiano-
   Reggiano cheese

2 tablespoons mayonnaise

2 teaspoons Dijon or German
   mustard

Note:

While a coating of panko undoubtedly provides crunch, I find that it rarely has enough time in the oven to get as golden brown as I want it to. Toasting the panko before it hits the oven guarantees a crisp, golden-brown coating no matter how long it bakes.

While many adventurous home cooks sing the praises of the roasted brined dish that is the star of their holiday meal, the idea of somehow emptying my fridge enough to have room for not just a giant bird but a giant bird in a giant vat is almost laughable. I mean, where do they expect me to put all my prosecco and cheese? That's why, when it comes to brining, pork is my protein of choice. Brining firms up pork chops while adding tons of juiciness and flavor in relatively short order. These are made all the better with a crisp coating reminiscent of a rhyming childhood favorite.

For the brine, in a deep bowl or square baking pan, whisk 1 cup of water with the salt, sugar, peppercorns, and garlic until the salt and sugar are dissolved. Stir in the cold lager then add the pork chops, ensuring they are submerged. Cover the bowl or pan with plastic wrap and refrigerate for 4 hours or up to overnight.

Preheat your oven to 425°F, spray a baking sheet with nonstick cooking spray, and remove the pork from the brine. Dry the pork with paper towel and set aside to come up to room temperature while you prepare the coating.

For the coating, melt the butter in a large skillet set over medium heat. Add the breadcrumbs, garlic powder, thyme, salt, paprika, cayenne pepper, and onion powder and toast, stirring frequently, until golden brown, 2 to 3 minutes. Transfer the breadcrumb mixture to a shallow dish and set aside to cool. Stir in the Parmigiano-Reggiano and set aside.

In a small bowl, stir together the mayonnaise and mustard.

Brush the pork chops with a thin layer of the mayo mixture, making sure to coat the sides as well. Press the chops into the panko mixture to evenly coat on all sides, then transfer to the prepared sheet pan.

Roast the pork for 15 to 18 minutes or until the internal temperature reaches 145°F or is cooked to your liking.

Cider Pork Tenderloin with Autumn Veg

SERVES 5 TO 6

BANG FOR
YOUR BUCK

FAST
FLAVOR

ONE
POT-ISH

2 pork tenderloins

1 tablespoon olive oil

Kosher salt

Freshly ground black pepper

1 tablespoon butter

1 red onion, cut into thin
wedges

1 small butternut squash,
peeled and cut into
1-inch dice

2 crisp apples, cored and sliced
into 10 to 12 wedges each

3 teaspoons finely chopped
rosemary, divided

3 teaspoons finely chopped
sage, divided

1 tablespoon maple syrup

2 tablespoons stone-ground
or Dijon mustard

½ teaspoon ground cinnamon

½ cup dry hard cider or dry
white wine

½ cup low-sodium chicken
broth

Note:

Swap the butternut squash
with diced sweet potatoes
or another hearty winter
squash. You can also use
regular potatoes or mini
potatoes but, as they are
denser than squash, you will
want to parboil them until
fork-tender before adding
to the pan.

Pork tenderloin is one of my favorite budget-friendly mains. It's casual enough for a Tuesday night while still fancy enough to impress, and it's flavorful, quick-cooking, and frequently on sale in my neck of the woods. By jazzing it up with autumn veg and flavors, this cozy one-pot dish is a regular in my kitchen.

Preheat your oven to 425°F and place a large cast-iron skillet over medium-high heat.

Using a piece of paper towel, pat the pork tenderloins dry and drizzle with oil. Season liberally with salt and pepper and sear the pork tenderloins until evenly browned all over, 2 to 3 minutes per side.

Transfer the pork to a plate, turn the heat down to medium, and add the butter to the pan. Add the onion and squash, season with salt and pepper, and cook for about 5 minutes or until lightly golden, stirring occasionally.

Add the apples along with 1½ teaspoons each of the rosemary and sage and continue to cook for 3 to 5 minutes, until the apples are lightly caramelized.

Meanwhile, in a small bowl, combine the maple syrup, mustard, cinnamon, and remaining 1½ teaspoons each of rosemary and sage. Brush onto the seared pork. Carefully deglaze the pan with the cider, making sure to scrape up any browned bits, and nestle the pork in among the veg.

Roast the pork for 15 to 17 minutes or until the internal temperature of the pork reaches 145°F.

Transfer the pork to a cutting board, cover it with foil, and allow it to rest for 5 to 8 minutes. Place the pan of veg over medium-low heat and add the chicken broth. Using a wooden spoon, scrape up any additional browned bits from the bottom of the pan and allow it to cook down slightly until ready to serve.

Thickly slice the pork and serve alongside the roasted veg with the pan sauce spooned over top.

French Onion Pot Roast with Gruyère Potatoes

SERVES 6 TO 8

GET
AHEAD

ONE
POT-ISH

SIMPLY
SNAZZY

FOR THE ROAST

3 lb chuck roast

Kosher salt

Freshly ground black pepper

1 tablespoon olive oil

2 tablespoons butter

8 yellow onions, thinly sliced

3 garlic cloves, chopped

1½ teaspoons packed
    brown sugar

¼ cup brandy

1 tablespoon all-purpose flour

2½–3 cups low-sodium beef
    broth

4 sprigs thyme

2 bay leaves

FOR THE POTATOES

2½ lb yellow potatoes, peeled
    and quartered

4 garlic cloves

4 sprigs thyme

Kosher salt

6 tablespoons butter

½ cup heavy cream

¼ cup buttermilk

7 oz Gruyère cheese, grated

3½ oz mozzarella cheese,
    grated

The ultimate low and slow comfort staple with a little *je ne sais quoi*, this recipe is one of my favorite make-aheads that, even after a few days, I'd happily serve to company (yes, even the mashed potatoes!). The sweetness of caramelized onions paired with rich and hearty slow-cooked beef is made all the more indulgent when paired with ultra cheesy, very French-feeling mashed potatoes.

Preheat your oven to 300°F.

For the roast, place a Dutch oven over medium-high heat. Using paper towel, dry off the outside of the roast and season well with salt and pepper. Add the oil to the pan and sear the roast until golden brown all over, 3 to 5 minutes per side. Remove the roast to a baking sheet or large bowl to catch any juices and set aside.

Turn the heat down to low, add the butter and onions, and season with salt and pepper. Cook for 20 to 25 minutes or until the onions are cooked down and golden, stirring occasionally. Stir in the garlic and sugar and increase the heat to medium. Cook for 5 to 10 minutes, stirring frequently, until deeply golden brown and well caramelized.

Deglaze the pan with brandy and allow to cook away for 1 to 2 minutes. Sprinkle the flour over the onions and stir well to combine. While stirring, slowly pour in 2½ cups of beef broth. Add the roast back to the pan and, if needed, add more beef broth to come halfway up the roast. Stir in the thyme and bay leaves and turn the heat up to medium-high and bring to a simmer.

Place the lid on the pan and transfer the roast to the oven for 3 to 3½ hours or until the roast is fork tender. When tender, remove the roast from the oven, leave the lid on, and set aside to rest while you make the potatoes.

continued

This pot roast is equally delicious spooned over a bowl of polenta. Just whip up a double batch of my Basic Polenta (recipe on page 248) and finish with Gruyère and mozzarella.

For the potatoes, place the potatoes in a pot and cover with cold water. Add the garlic and thyme, generously season with salt, and bring to a boil over medium-high heat. Cook the potatoes until fork tender, 15 to 20 minutes. Drain, discard the thyme, and return the potatoes and garlic to the pot.

Roughly mash the potatoes and garlic with a masher and add the butter, cream, and buttermilk. Using a hand mixer, beat the potatoes until smooth and creamy. Switch to a heatproof spatula or wooden spoon and gradually begin stirring in the grated Gruyère and mozzarella, adding about a handful at a time. Season the potatoes with salt to taste and, if needed, add a splash more cream or buttermilk until the potatoes reach your desired consistency.

Using tongs or two forks, pull the beef apart into large chunks and serve over the cheesy mashed potatoes with a few ladlefuls of the onion gravy.

If you're looking to get ahead, you can store the beef, gravy and all, in the Dutch oven and transfer the potatoes to a greased baking dish. Cover and keep in the fridge for up to 3 days.

To reheat, leave the beef covered and place over medium-low heat. Uncover the potatoes and transfer to a 375°F oven. Cook both for 35 to 45 minutes or until heated through and the potatoes are lightly golden brown and crisp around the edges.

Bacon-Wrapped Meatloaf

SERVES 6 TO 8

½ lb regular cut bacon,
about 9 slices

1 tablespoon olive oil

2 yellow onions, finely diced

1 teaspoon dried thyme

Kosher salt

Freshly ground black pepper

2 garlic cloves, finely grated

2 tablespoons Worcestershire
sauce

3 slices sandwich bread,
crusts removed

½ cup milk

2.2 lb extra-lean ground beef

¼ cup finely chopped parsley

2 eggs

1 tablespoon ketchup

2 teaspoons Dijon mustard

Meatloaf is one of those ultra-retro dishes that hasn't changed all that much over the years. Recipes today look much the same as those that my nana would have made, and while that's not a bad thing at all, I do think there is some room for improvement in the world of meatloaf. By wrapping the outside in bacon, this not only gives your meatloaf a smoky, bacony flavor, It helps hold in the juices that can often bleed out while cooking. The final step of turning it out and crisping it in the oven ensures a juicy interior and perfect golden-brown exterior.

Preheat your oven to 350°F and line a standard loaf pan with two slings of parchment paper. Lay the bacon into the pan so that it overlaps, lining the bottom and longer sides. Set the pan aside in the fridge.

Place a sauté pan over medium heat. Add the oil, onions, and thyme, season with salt and pepper, and cook until soft and lightly golden, 5 to 7 minutes. Stir in the garlic and continue to cook for 1 minute, then deglaze the pan with the Worcestershire sauce and set aside to cool completely.

Meanwhile, tear the bread into small pieces and place in a small bowl. Pour in the milk and mix well to combine. Set aside to allow the bread to soak up the milk. You want the bread to break down into a less-than-appetizing-looking paste. This should take 8 to 10 minutes.

In a large bowl, combine the beef, parsley, eggs, ketchup, and mustard with the cooled onions and bread mixture. Season with salt and pepper. Using two forks or your fingers like rakes, blend the mixture together. You don't want to press or squeeze the mixture, as that will lead to a tough meatloaf. Retrieve the prepared loaf pan from the fridge and place onto a sheet pan in case of any boil-over

Add the meatloaf mixture to the prepared pan, gently pressing it into a loaf shape. Fold over the overhanging bacon and bake for 45 minutes.

continued

Remove the meatloaf and sheet pan from the oven, set the meatloaf aside, increase the temperature of your oven to 400°F, and line the sheet pan with aluminum foil, dull side up. Place the sheet pan foil side down onto the loaf pan and carefully and quickly turn the meatloaf out. Remove the loaf pan and parchment paper and return the meatloaf to the oven for 15 to 20 minutes or until the bacon is crisp and the internal temperature of the meatloaf reaches 160°F.

Allow the meatloaf to rest for at least 10 minutes before slicing and serving.

Leftovers will keep in an airtight container in the fridge for up to 3 days. To freeze leftovers, slice the meatloaf, divide each piece with parchment, wax paper, or aluminum foil, and store in a freezer bag for up to 3 months. Defrost the meatloaf in the microwave or in the fridge overnight before reheating.

Note:

A panade is the secret to perfectly moist and tender meatloaf. Also used in things like meatballs, this pasty mixture of bread-crumbs and milk (or other liquids) gives body to ground meat mixtures and helps them hold onto fats and moisture that tend to bleed out while cooking.

Reverse-Sear Steak with Chimichurri

SERVES 4

One 2–2.2 lb rib eye, T-bone,
or porterhouse steak, about
2 inches thick

3 tablespoons red wine
vinegar

½ shallot, finely minced

2 garlic cloves, finely grated

½ cup finely chopped cilantro

¼ cup finely chopped parsley

1 tablespoon finely chopped
oregano

½ teaspoon crushed red
pepper flakes

¼ cup extra virgin olive oil

Kosher salt

Note:

If you want to try a reverse
sear with a less pricey cut
of beef, be sure to use a
cut that is at least 1¼ inches
thick and don't forget
about that digital probe
thermometer. The thinner
the cut, the quicker it will
come up to temperature in
the oven, so it is the only
way to ensure a perfect
cook every single time.

Being a go-to person for food-related questions is one of my favorite aspects of my job. So when my friend Sarah asked about reverse searing steak, oooh baby, was I ever pumped! She doesn't cook a lot, and I was so proud of her for wanting to try something new! After a few hasty text instructions, she was well on her way. Cut to a few hours later, she sent a picture of the most perfectly cooked steak I've ever seen. While it technically takes more forethought than just throwing a steak on the grill, this method is the best way to ensure perfectly cooked steak every single time, no matter your skill level.

Place the steak on a baking sheet lined with a wire rack, and set on the counter for 2 hours before cooking to allow it to come up to room temperature. This step is critical for reverse searing.

Meanwhile, in a small glass, ceramic, or plastic bowl, combine the vinegar, shallot, garlic, cilantro, parsley, oregano, red pepper flakes, and oil, and season with ¾ teaspoon of salt. Stir well and set aside in the fridge.

Preheat your oven to 250°F and dry off the outside of the steak with paper towel. Season generously with salt and pepper.

Cook the steak in the low oven until the internal temperature reaches 105°F for rare, about 25 minutes, or 115°F for medium-rare, 30 to 35 minutes, being sure to check the temperature often as cooking times can vary depending on the thickness of your steak, its temperature when it went into the oven, and your oven's consistency. For ease, I suggest using a leave-in digital probe thermometer with a temperature alarm.

Meanwhile, heat your grill or a cast-iron skillet to high.

When the steak is up to temperature, transfer it to the grill or skillet and sear until golden and charred on both sides, 2 to 3 minutes total.

With this slower cooking method, you do not have to let the steak rest. Simply cut the steak from the bone, if needed, slice into about ½-inch-thick pieces, and serve with the chimichurri.

Roast Beef Bourguignon

SERVES 4 TO 6

FOR THE BEEF

4 lb prime rib roast (see note)

3 tablespoons butter, room
    temperature

1½ teaspoons herbes
    de Provence

Kosher salt

Freshly cracked black pepper

FOR THE SAUCE

3 slices regular cut bacon,
    diced

8 oz cremini mushrooms,
    halved or quartered

Kosher salt

Freshly ground black pepper

1 teaspoon finely chopped
    thyme

¾ cup drained cocktail onions

2 garlic cloves, finely grated

2 tablespoons butter

2 tablespoons all-purpose
    flour

1 tablespoon tomato paste

¾ cup dry red wine, preferably
    Burgundy

1½ cups low-sodium beef broth

1 teaspoon packed brown
    sugar

2 tablespoons finely chopped
    parsley

Whenever I'm spending a lot of money on an ingredient, it has to make at least one of my jobs in the kitchen easier. Whether it saves on dishes or requires less effort or time, it needs to do a good amount of heavy lifting for me. With this prime rib recipe, while it takes a little forethought and a relatively long time in the oven, the roast itself involves little to no effort, giving you more than enough time to make a quick bourguignon-inspired sauce. This recipe looks wordy, but it's a cinch to make.

For the beef, the day or night before you are going to cook and serve the roast, unwrap the beef, dry it off with a piece of paper towel, and place onto a small baking sheet or roasting pan lined with a wire rack. For easier cleanup, line the pan with aluminum foil. Return the roast to the fridge and allow it to sit uncovered for at least 8 hours. This process will greatly increase the roast's browning potential and help the flavorful butter stick to the outside.

Remove the roast from the fridge and place it on the counter for at least 2 hours or up to 4 hours to come up to room temperature.

Preheat your oven to 500°F and, once heated, set a timer for 30 minutes. With the oven sear method, you want your oven to be smoking hot, and allowing it to sit at temperature for half an hour will help ensure a good golden-brown color.

Meanwhile, in a small bowl, combine the butter and herbes de Provence. Spread the butter all over the roast and season well with salt and pepper. If using a digital probe thermometer (and I do highly recommend using one), insert it into the center of the roast, avoiding the rib bones if using a bone-in roast, and set the temperature alarm for 130°F. Transfer the roast to the oven and set a timer for 20 minutes for a 4 lb roast (if your roast weighs more or less than 4 lb, see the note to calculate the cooking time). When the timer goes off, turn the oven off and set another timer for 2 hours. Without opening the oven door, allow the roast to sit in the oven for the full 2 hours, or until the probe thermometer reaches 130°F.

continued

In the last 30 minutes of roasting, prepare the sauce.

Place the bacon in a large skillet set over medium heat and cook until crisp, about 5 minutes. Remove the bacon to a plate, leaving the fat behind, and add the mushrooms. Season with salt and pepper and cook until lightly golden, about 5 minutes, stirring occasionally. Add the thyme and cocktail onions, and continue to cook until the mushrooms are golden brown and the onions pick up a little color, about another 5 minutes. Add the garlic and cook for 30 seconds, then transfer the mushroom mixture to the plate with the bacon and set aside.

Place the pan back over medium heat, melt in the butter, and sprinkle in the flour. Whisk together, then add the tomato paste and cook for about 1 minute. While whisking, slowly pour in the wine followed by the beef broth. Bring the mixture to a simmer and cook for 5 minutes to thicken slightly. Add the sugar as well as the mushrooms, onions, and bacon to the sauce and simmer for 2 to 3 minutes to thicken and heat through. Season to taste with salt and pepper, stir in the parsley, and turn the heat down to low to keep warm.

When the timer or thermometer goes off, remove the roast from the oven. Cut off the ribs, if using a bone-in roast, and slice. Like with a reverse-sear method, this oven-off cooking method does not require resting the roast before serving. Serve the roast topped with the bourguignon sauce.

Note:

This oven-off cooking method can be used for any good beef roast weighing between 3 and 8 lb—all you need is a calculator to figure out the initial cooking time. The simple formula is its weight in pounds times 5 equals the number of minutes your roast is in the oven before turning off the heat. If the answer has any decimal points, just round the number to the nearest whole (for example, if your roast weighs 3.5 lb, you would roast it for 18 minutes before turning the oven off [3.5 lb × 5 = 17.5, rounded up to 18]). No matter the size of the roast, it will stay in the oven for 2 hours after you turn the oven off.

Sweets

GET
AHEAD

GREAT
GIFTING

WEEKNIGHT
BAKING

My Dream Chocolate Chip Cookie

MAKES 18 LARGE COOKIES

¾ cup unsalted butter,
  room temperature, divided

¾ cup packed brown sugar

¾ cup granulated sugar

2 eggs

1½ teaspoons vanilla extract

2 cups all-purpose flour

2 teaspoons cornstarch

1½ teaspoons baking soda

½ teaspoon kosher salt

7 oz semi-sweet chocolate
  chunks

Flaky sea salt, optional

Note:

The small amount of cornstarch in this cookie dough helps soften the proteins in the flour, keeping the middle of each cookie nice and chewy.

If you're making these ahead, you can place the scooped dough into the fridge for 2 hours until firm, then transfer to a resealable bag and store in the fridge for up to 1 day or in the freezer for up to 3 months. Bake the cookies straight from the fridge or freezer as directed.

I'm a pretty low-maintenance gal when it comes to my chocolate chip cookie demands. I want it to be thin but not too thin, crispy around the edges, chewy in the middle but *not* because it's undercooked, and perfectly salty/sweet, and I want it to keep that fresh-baked flavor and texture for more than a few hours. All right, so maybe I'm not the easiest to please, but that's why it's taken me so long to come out with my very own "Mary Berg–approved" chocolate chip cookie recipe.

Preheat your oven to 350°F and line a baking sheet with parchment paper.

In a small skillet set over medium heat, melt ¼ cup butter and bring to a simmer. Allow the butter to cook for 1 to 2 minutes, stirring frequently, until golden-brown flecks appear. Immediately transfer the browned butter to a large bowl or the bowl of your stand mixer and set aside to cool. As this is such a small amount of butter, it both browns and cools relatively quickly.

Add the remaining ½ cup of butter to the bowl along with both sugars and cream on high until well combined and a little lighter in color, about 3 minutes. Add the eggs one at a time, beating well after each addition. Beat in the vanilla and set aside.

In a separate bowl, whisk together the flour, cornstarch, baking soda, and salt. Stir in the chocolate and add the dry ingredients to the butter and sugar mixture. Beat just until combined.

Using a 2 oz ice cream scoop or a large tablespoon, scoop the cookie dough onto the lined baking sheet, leaving at least 4 inches between each cookie. Sprinkle with a pinch of flaky sea salt. You will have to bake these cookies in batches. For me, six cookies fit on a large baking sheet, so I bake them in three batches.

Bake the cookies for 12 to 14 minutes or until the edges are golden brown and the middles are still soft. Allow the cookies to sit on the baking sheet for 2 minutes before transferring to a wire rack to cool completely. Store cooled cookies at room temperature in a container or resealable bag for up to 5 days.

Ginger Molasses Cookies

MAKES 12 TO 14 LARGE COOKIES

½ cup unsalted butter,
 room temperature

½ cup packed brown sugar

½ cup granulated sugar

¼ cup molasses

1 egg

½ teaspoon vanilla extract

1 cup all-purpose flour

1 cup bread flour

2 teaspoons cornstarch

1½ teaspoons baking soda

¼ teaspoon kosher salt

1 teaspoon cinnamon

1 teaspoon ground ginger

¼ teaspoon ground cloves

1 cup turbinado sugar,
 for rolling

Note:

Brown sugar is just granulated sugar that has a little bit of molasses mixed in. You can easily make your own by combining 1 cup of granulated sugar with 1 tablespoon of molasses for light brown sugar or 2 tablespoons for dark brown sugar. Use a hand mixer or a food processor for easy mixing.

When I first met Aaron, he was playing in bands that would go on cross-country tours a couple of times per year. My mom always wanted to send him off with a taste of home, as he packed into a van with his bandmates and all their gear looking forward to a month of fast food. She would bake up triple batches of these ginger molasses cookies, wrap them up in zip-top freezer bags, and send them along to take the guys through at least that first leg of the tour. Perfectly chewy, wonderfully warm and spicy, these cookies stay fresh for at least a week, making them the perfect thing to fuel the Canadian indie music scene.

Preheat the oven to 350°F and line two large baking sheets with parchment paper.

In a large bowl or the bowl of your stand mixer, cream together the butter and both sugars until light and creamy, scraping down the bowl at least once midway through. Add the molasses and beat together, followed by the egg and vanilla extract, scraping the bowl at least once.

In a separate bowl, sift together the all-purpose flour, bread flour, cornstarch, baking soda, salt, cinnamon, ginger, and cloves. Add the dry ingredients to the wet and mix just until combined.

Sprinkle the turbinado sugar into a shallow dish and, using a 2 oz ice cream scoop or large tablespoon, scoop the cookie dough into the sugar. Toss to coat the dough with the sugar and place the cookies onto the prepared baking sheets, about 4 inches apart.

Bake the cookies one sheet at a time for 14 to 16 minutes or until the edges are set. Allow them to cool on the baking sheet for 5 minutes, then transfer to a wire rack to cool completely.

Store the cooled cookies at room temperature in a container or resealable bag for up to 1 week.

If you're making these ahead, you can place the sugar-coated dough into the fridge for 2 hours until firm, then transfer to a resealable bag and store in the fridge for up to 1 day or in the freezer for up to 3 months. Bake the cookies straight from the fridge or freezer as directed.

Whatever You Like Slice & Bake Cookies

MAKES 4 DOZEN

GET
AHEAD

GREAT
GIFTING

WEEKNIGHT
BAKING

1¼ cups unsalted butter, room temperature

¾ cup packed dark brown sugar

¼ cup granulated sugar

2 teaspoons vanilla extract

1 egg white

2¾ cups all-purpose flour

1 teaspoon kosher salt

¼ teaspoon baking soda

If the idea of a holiday cookie exchange sends shivers up your spine, these are the cookies for you. This versatile dough can be flavored with different extracts, zests, and mix-ins (see the next page for some of my favorite combos), and as the dough stores so well in the freezer, you can either get way ahead and have all your holiday baking done by the end of September or have fresh cookies all the way into March.

In a large bowl or the bowl of your stand mixer, cream together the butter and both sugars until light and fluffy, about 2 minutes. Add the vanilla extract and egg white and beat well to combine.

In a separate bowl, whisk together the flour, salt, and baking soda.

Add the dry ingredients to the butter and sugar mixture and mix just until combined.

Divide the cookie dough into four equal pieces and roll each into a 5-inch log. Wrap each log in plastic wrap and chill the cookie dough for at least 2 hours in the refrigerator or place in the freezer for up to 3 months.

Preheat your oven to 350°F and line a baking sheet with parchment paper. If the cookie dough is frozen, place it on the counter for 10 minutes while your oven heats up to make slicing easier. Slice each log into twelve equal rounds and place on the baking sheet, leaving at least 3 inches of space between each.

Bake the cookies for 12 to 15 minutes or until lightly golden around the edge. Remove from the oven and allow the cookies to rest on the baking sheet for 2 minutes before transferring to a wire rack to cool completely. Store the cookies in an airtight container at room temperature for up to 5 days.

continued

A few of my favorite flavor combinations

LEMON ALMOND

Add the zest of one lemon and ½ teaspoon almond extract to the butter and sugar mixture. When combining the dry ingredients, stir in ½ cup finely chopped white chocolate and ¼ cup chopped almonds.

SPICE

Stir ½ teaspoon each of cinnamon and ginger, along with ¼ teaspoon each of cloves and nutmeg into the dry ingredients. Roll the logs of cookie dough in ½ cup of turbinado sugar, pressing to adhere, before placing in the fridge or freezer.

CHOCOLATE ORANGE

Add the zest of one orange to the butter and sugar mixture. When combining the dry ingredients, stir in ¼ cup mini semi-sweet chocolate chips or finely chopped semi-sweet chocolate, ¼ cup finely chopped pecans, and ¼ cup finely chopped dried cranberries.

MOCHA

Stir 1 teaspoon instant espresso powder into the vanilla extract before adding it to the butter and sugar mixture. Replace ¼ cup of the all-purpose flour with ¼ cup of cocoa powder. Top each cookie with a chocolate-covered espresso bean, then bake.

Note:

If making a chocolate cookie base with this recipe, you can replace ¼ cup of the flour with ¼ cup of cocoa powder. However, this 1:1 ratio does not work with all recipes, so I wouldn't apply it as a general rule.

Raspberry Cheesecake Blondies

MAKES 9 LARGE SQUARES

1 cup unsalted butter,
  room temperature

2¼ cups all-purpose flour

1½ teaspoons baking powder

1 teaspoon kosher salt

1 cup packed brown sugar

½ cup + 3 tablespoons
  granulated sugar, divided

2 large eggs, room
  temperature

3 teaspoons vanilla extract,
  divided

1 cup brick-style cream cheese,
  room temperature

1 cup fresh raspberries

Even though I cook and write recipes pretty much every single day, I still mess up. But that's just part of life, baby! When I was working out this particular recipe, things started going sideways almost immediately. The blondie batter was weird and lumpy, the cheesecake mixture was thin and eggy, and, to top it all off, I dumped it into the wrong-sized pan. After a few more attempts, I finally nailed it. This is not only the perfect square but also happens to be the easiest version in a string of overly complicated, albeit delicious, trash.

Preheat your oven to 350°F and grease a 9-inch square baking pan with nonstick cooking spray.

In a small pot set over medium heat, melt the butter and bring to a simmer. Allow the butter to cook for 5 to 7 minutes, stirring frequently, until golden-brown flecks appear. Immediately transfer the browned butter to a large bowl and set aside to cool slightly.

Meanwhile, whisk together the flour, baking powder, and salt and set aside.

When the butter has cooled slightly, beat in the brown sugar and ½ cup of the granulated sugar until well combined. Beat in the eggs, one at a time, and stir in 2 teaspoons of the vanilla. Add the dry ingredients to the brown butter mixture and mix just until combined. Spread the batter into the prepared baking pan and set aside.

In the same bowl, beat the cream cheese with the remaining 3 tablespoons of granulated sugar and 1 teaspoon of vanilla until smooth and creamy. Dot the cream cheese mixture over the blondie batter and scatter the raspberries overtop. Using a butter knife, gently swirl everything together. Since both batters are on the thicker side, it will look like a bit of a mess, the raspberries will get broken up, and the top will be rumpled, but that's OK. It will bake up beautifully.

Bake for 40 to 45 minutes or until the edges are golden brown and the middle is set.

continued

Allow the blondies to cool slightly before slicing and serving. They can also be served at room temperature.

Store leftover blondies in an airtight container or zip-top bag at room temperature for up to 1 day or in the fridge for up to 5 days. If storing in the fridge, let them sit at room temperature for 15 minutes before eating for optimal texture.

Note:

Brown butter gives baked goods that fresh-baked flavor long after they've come out of the oven. But if the idea of browning butter isn't in your wheelhouse today, just use melted butter.

GET
AHEAD

GREAT
GIFTING

WEEKNIGHT
BAKING

Marble Zucchini Loaf
with Chocolate Cinnamon Streusel

MAKES 1 LOAF

FOR THE LOAF

1 cup granulated sugar

½ cup + 2 tablespoons
    canola oil, divided

2 eggs

¼ cup buttermilk

1 teaspoon vanilla extract

1½ cups grated zucchini,
    about 1 medium zucchini

1¾ cups all-purpose flour

1 teaspoon cinnamon

¼ teaspoon ground ginger

1 teaspoon baking powder

½ teaspoon baking soda

½ teaspoon kosher salt

3 tablespoons cocoa powder

FOR THE STREUSEL

¼ cup packed brown sugar

3 tablespoons all-purpose flour

1 tablespoon cocoa powder

1 teaspoon cinnamon

¼ teaspoon kosher salt

3 tablespoons melted butter

The first time I tried tackling a marble cake recipe, I thought the only option was to simultaneously make two completely different cake batters then swirl them together. There are many reasons why that was a silly assumption, from viscosity issues and baking time differences to conflicting leavening agents and just the stress of making two cakes, but the moral of the story is that you get to learn from my mistake. By making just one batter then mixing half with some cocoa power and oil, you get all the flavors of two batters for the effort of one.

Preheat your oven to 350°F and grease a standard 5-by-9-inch loaf pan with nonstick cooking spray.

For the loaf, in a large bowl, whisk the sugar with ½ cup of the oil, the eggs, buttermilk, and vanilla until well combined. Stir in the grated zucchini and set aside.

In a separate bowl, stir together the flour, cinnamon, ginger, baking powder, baking soda, and salt. Add the dry ingredients to the wet and stir just until combined.

In a medium bowl, whisk together the cocoa powder with the remaining 2 tablespoons of oil. Scoop about half of the batter into the cocoa mixture and stir just to combine.

Alternating batters, scoop into the prepared loaf pan in a rough checkerboard pattern. Using a butter knife, slightly swirl the batters together to create a marbled effect and set the pan aside while you make the streusel topping.

For the streusel, in a small bowl, combine the brown sugar, flour, cocoa powder, cinnamon, and salt. Pour the butter overtop and, using a spoon or your fingers, mix until crumbly and combined.

Scatter the streusel over the batter and bake for 50 minutes to 1 hour or until deeply golden brown and a cake tester or skewer inserted into the center of the loaf comes out clean.

Allow the loaf to cool in the pan for at least 20 minutes before turning it out onto a wire rack to cool completely. Store the loaf tightly wrapped at room temperature for up to 3 days.

Note: If you're looking to increase fiber in your baking, whole wheat flour is the obvious choice, but whole wheat flour is heavier and absorbs more water than all-purpose flour. That means that if you were to substitute all the flour for whole wheat, you'd end up with a very dense, very dry loaf. To maintain texture, try substituting up to a third of the all-purpose flour called for in a recipe for whole wheat. In this loaf, try 1¼ cups all-purpose and ½ cup of whole wheat.

Coconut Loaf with Chocolate Hazelnut Glaze

MAKES 1 BUNDT CAKE

GREAT
GIFTING

WEEKNIGHT
BAKING

1½ cups unsalted butter,
   room temperature

2 cups granulated sugar

2 cups shredded unsweetened
   coconut

6 eggs

¾ cup sour cream or yogurt
   (plain, vanilla, or coconut)

2 teaspoons vanilla extract

1½ teaspoons coconut extract

3 cups all-purpose flour

1½ teaspoons baking powder

¾ teaspoon kosher salt

1½ cups chocolate hazelnut
   spread

Toasted coconut, optional,
   for garnish

Note:

The "one at a time" rule for
adding eggs to baking has to
do with emulsification. Similar
to making mayonnaise or a
salad dressing, you're trying
to incorporate something with
a relatively high water content
(eggs) into something with a
high fat content (butter and
sugar). By adding the eggs
one at a time and mixing well
after each addition, you can
help ensure a smooth batter
that will not curdle or split.

This may be a controversial opinion, but I don't particularly care for frostings and buttercreams on my cakes. When there is something perfectly creamy, spreadable, nutty, and chocolaty sitting right in my pantry, why go to the trouble?

Preheat your oven to 325°F and lightly grease a Bundt or tube pan with nonstick cooking spray.

In a large bowl or the bowl of your stand mixer, beat the butter and sugar on high speed for 6 to 7 minutes until light and fluffy.

Meanwhile, place a skillet over medium-low heat and add the coconut to toast, stirring frequently. This should take 1 to 2 minutes. Transfer the coconut from the pan and set aside to cool.

Return to the butter and sugar mixture, scrape down the bowl, and beat in the eggs, one at a time, until combined. Stir in the sour cream along with the vanilla and coconut extracts and set aside.

In a separate bowl, whisk the flour, baking powder, and salt together. Stir in the cooled coconut, then add the dry ingredients all at once to the butter mixture. Stir just until combined.

Transfer the batter to the prepared pan and bake for 1 hour and 15 minutes or until risen and springy and a toothpick inserted into the center comes out clean. Cool the loaf in the pan for 20 minutes, then turn out onto a wire rack to cool completely to room temperature.

When cool, heat the chocolate hazelnut spread in the microwave for 10 to 20 seconds or in a small saucepan over low heat for 1 to 2 minutes just until slightly warm. Pour over the cake, allowing it to drip down the sides, scatter with toasted coconut, if using, then slice and serve.

Store the cake covered at room temperature for up to 3 days.

Lemon Cornmeal Olive Oil Cake

MAKES ONE 9-INCH CAKE

FOR THE CAKE

1 tablespoon + ½ cup yellow
    cornmeal, divided

1 cup packed brown sugar

½ cup olive oil

2 eggs

1 cup plain yogurt

1 lemon, zested and juiced

1½ teaspoons vanilla extract

1½ cups all-purpose flour

1 teaspoon baking powder

1 teaspoon baking soda

½ teaspoon kosher salt

1 cup lemon curd, store-bought
    or homemade, recipe follows

FOR THE RICOTTA
WHIPPED CREAM

1 cup 35% whipping cream

½ cup ricotta

1 tablespoon granulated sugar
    or honey

½ teaspoon vanilla extract

1 lemon

Note:

If you happen to be a batter
eater, don't be alarmed by
how strong the olive oil flavor
is. The flavor will mellow as
the cake bakes, leaving you
with a subtle savory olive oil
flavor that pairs beautifully
with the lemon.

A straightforward showstopper, this super flavorful cake can be made with store-bought lemon curd to keep things easy breezy. If you're feeling slightly more ambitious, homemade lemon curd is almost as simple as boiling water—see my recipe on the next page.

Preheat your oven to 350°F and spray a 9-inch springform pan with nonstick cooking spray. Sprinkle in 1 tablespoon of cornmeal and shake the pan to evenly coat the bottom and sides, tapping out any excess.

For the cake, in a large bowl or the bowl of your stand mixer, beat together the brown sugar, oil, and eggs until well combined. Stir in the yogurt, lemon zest, lemon juice, and vanilla, and set aside.

In a separate bowl, whisk the remaining ½ cup of cornmeal with the flour, baking powder, baking soda, and salt. Add the dry ingredients to the oil and sugar mixture and stir just until combined. Set the batter aside for 20 minutes to allow the cornmeal to hydrate.

Pour the batter into the prepared pan. Using a small spoon, scoop dots of lemon curd over the batter, then swirl it in using a butter knife or bamboo skewer.

Bake for 40 to 45 minutes or until the center of the cake is springy and a toothpick inserted into the middle, avoiding the lemon curd, comes out clean. If there is a little lemon curd on the toothpick, that is fine. You just don't want any cake batter. Allow the cake to cool for 15 minutes, then turn the cake out onto a wire rack to cool completely.

When the cake is cool, make the ricotta whipped cream. Whip the cream, ricotta, sugar, vanilla, and the zest of half of the lemon on medium speed until stiff peaks form, 2 to 3 minutes. Dollop or spread the ricotta whipped cream over the cooled cake and scatter the zest of the remaining lemon half overtop.

Slice and serve with an extra spoonful of lemon curd, if desired.

If you are making the cake in advance, leave it untopped, tightly wrapped in plastic wrap, at room temperature for up to 4 days. Once topped, store the cake covered in the fridge for up to 2 days.

continued

Simple Lemon Curd

MAKES ABOUT 1 CUP

1 tablespoon lemon zest,
  about 1 lemon

⅓ cup lemon juice, about
  2 lemons

⅓ cup granulated sugar

¼ teaspoon kosher salt

2 eggs

1 tablespoon butter

Whisk the lemon zest, lemon juice, sugar, salt, and eggs together in a small saucepot and cook over medium heat, stirring frequently, until thick, 2 to 4 minutes. Whisk in the butter and remove the curd from the heat. Pass the curd through a fine-mesh sieve into a resealable container, and chill in the fridge until needed. Lemon curd will keep in the fridge for 1 week.

Tiramisu Cupcakes

MAKES 1 DOZEN CUPCAKES

DINNER
PARTY
DESSERT

WEEKEND
PROJECT

FOR THE CUPCAKES

½ cup unsalted butter,
    room temperature

½ cup granulated sugar

½ cup packed brown sugar

2 large eggs

2 teaspoons vanilla extract

1 cup sour cream

2 cups all-purpose flour

1½ teaspoons baking powder

1 teaspoon baking soda

½ teaspoon kosher salt

FOR THE COFFEE SYRUP

¼ cup brewed coffee

¼ cup granulated sugar

2 teaspoons marsala wine
    or dark rum, optional

½ teaspoon vanilla extract

FOR THE MASCARPONE CREAM

1 cup mascarpone cheese

1 cup icing sugar

½ cup 35% whipping cream

1 tablespoon marsala wine
    or dark rum, optional

1 teaspoon vanilla extract

Cocoa powder, for dusting

Tiramisu is one of those desserts that looks much simpler than it actually is. While the ladyfingers and coffee syrup are a relative cinch, the sugary egg yolk and marsala wine layer can quickly go from smooth and creamy to a sweet scrambled-egg mess. To prevent this mishap without giving up the delicious coffee-rich flavor of homemade tiramisu, give these cupcakes a try.

Preheat your oven to 350°F and lightly grease a 12-cup muffin tin with nonstick cooking spray.

For the cupcakes, in a large bowl or the bowl of your stand mixer, beat the butter and sugars together until pale and fluffy, 3 to 4 minutes. Add the eggs one at a time, beating well after each addition, then stir in the vanilla and sour cream.

In a separate bowl, whisk together the flour, baking powder, baking soda, and salt. Add the dry ingredients to the wet and stir just to combine. Using two spoons or a spring-loaded ice cream scoop, divide the batter into the prepared muffin tin.

Bake for 22 to 25 minutes or until a toothpick inserted into the center of a cupcake comes out clean. Set aside to cool.

Meanwhile, make the coffee syrup by combining the coffee and sugar in a small saucepan and bringing to a simmer over medium heat. Stir until the sugar is dissolved, 2 to 3 minutes, then remove from the heat and stir in the marsala wine and vanilla. Using a fork, poke a few holes into the top of each cupcake and spoon or pour the warm coffee syrup overtop. Allow the cupcakes to soak up the syrup, then transfer to a wire rack to cool completely.

For the mascarpone cream, in the bowl of your stand mixer or in a large bowl using a hand mixer, beat the mascarpone and icing sugar together on medium speed until smooth. With the mixer running, slowly stream in the whipping cream and whip until smooth and fluffy, 1 to 2 minutes. Do not overbeat, as that will curdle the cream. Finally, beat in the marsala wine and vanilla.

continued

Dollop or pipe the mascarpone cream onto each cupcake and dust the tops with cocoa powder. The cupcakes will keep at room temperature for a few hours. If making the cupcakes in advance, the mascarpone cream does need to be refrigerated. Store the cream in a container in the fridge and the cupcakes covered at room temperature for up to 3 days and decorate just before serving.

Note:

If you don't have or cannot find mascarpone, substitute 1 cup of room-temperature brick-style cream cheese. The flavor will be slightly more tangy but still delicious.

Chocolate Peanut Butter Cake
with Cornflake Crunch

MAKES ONE 9-INCH CAKE

FOR THE CAKE

1 cup all-purpose flour

½ cup cocoa powder

1 cup sugar

1 teaspoon baking soda

½ teaspoon baking powder

½ teaspoon kosher salt

½ cup buttermilk

¼ cup canola oil

1 egg

1 teaspoon vanilla extract

½ cup hot black coffee

½ cup smooth peanut butter,
not natural

FOR THE CORNFLAKE CRUNCH

½ cup butterscotch or peanut
butter chips

1 cup cornflakes

¼ cup roasted peanuts,
coarsely chopped

¼ teaspoon flaky sea salt

**FOR THE PEANUT BUTTER
GANACHE**

¼ cup 35% whipping cream

4 oz milk chocolate, finely
chopped

2 tablespoons smooth peanut
butter, not natural

If you haven't noticed, there is a bit of a trend in this book with respect to cakes, and it is 100 percent influenced by my own tastes: single-layer cakes are where it's at. Sure, a multilayer number gets to shine on birthdays, but pretty much every other occasion is, in my opinion, best celebrated with what I call a "tea cake"—a deceptively subtle single-layer showpiece that wows with an "Oh, I just threw this together" nonchalance.

For the cake, preheat your oven to 350°F and grease a 9-inch round cake pan with nonstick cooking spray.

Sift the flour and cocoa powder into a large bowl. Whisk in the sugar, baking soda, baking powder, and salt until well combined. Add the buttermilk, oil, egg, and vanilla and whisk just to combine. Stir in the hot coffee and pour the batter into the prepared cake pan.

Heat the peanut butter in the microwave or over a double boiler until thin and liquid, drizzle over the cake batter, and swirl in with a butter knife.

Bake the cake for 30 to 35 minutes or until springy to the touch and a skewer inserted into the center comes out clean.

Allow the cake to cool in the pan for 20 minutes then turn out onto a wire rack to cool completely.

Meanwhile, make the cornflake crunch by melting the butterscotch or peanut butter chips in a large bowl in the microwave in 15-second bursts or by heating them over a double boiler. Stir in the cornflakes and peanuts and transfer to a piece of parchment, spreading the mixture into a clumpy but even layer. Sprinkle the top with the flaky sea salt and set aside to harden.

continued

Make the peanut butter ganache by heating the whipping cream in the microwave or in a pan over low heat until steamy but not yet simmering. Add the chopped chocolate to a bowl, pour the hot cream overtop, and set aside for 5 to 10 minutes to melt the chocolate. Whisk the mixture until well combined, then whisk in the peanut butter until smooth. Allow the ganache to cool slightly until it is a thick, pourable consistency.

Place the cake on a pedestal or serving plate and pour the ganache overtop, allowing it to drip down the sides. Break up the cornflake crunch and scatter overtop as well.

The cake can be served immediately or stored covered at room temperature for up to 3 days.

Note:

A happy accident while grocery shopping led to the surprise star of this cake. While perusing the baking aisle looking for peanut butter chips, I hastily grabbed a bag of butterscotch instead. Typically, I find butterscotch chips cloyingly sweet but, with the cornflakes, peanuts, and extra sprinkle of salt, oh my gosh, so good. While either will work, this is just further proof of my belief that there are no mistakes in the kitchen.

Basic Pastry

MAKES 1 SINGLE-CRUST PIE, EASILY DOUBLED FOR A DOUBLE-CRUST PIE

1¼ cups all-purpose flour

½ teaspoon kosher salt

½ cup unsalted butter, chilled
and cut into ½-inch cubes

4–6 tablespoons ice water

1 teaspoon white vinegar

4–5 cups dried beans,
if blind baking

For a recipe containing only a handful of pantry staple ingredients, this one looks *exhausting*. Even me, looking at this method, I'm like "Berg! Calm down!" But I wanted to write a thorough recipe for something that really scares a lot of home cooks: pastry. You can use this for either sweet or savory pies, and I'm here to walk you through every step, but if you're like TL:DR, I've pulled out the main points and listed them on page 217. But just remember, pastry is one of those recipes that will get better and easier the more you make it. So don't give up!

In a large bowl, stir together the flour and salt. Add the butter and, using your fingertips, smoosh and snap the butter into the flour, almost like you're counting out Monopoly money. Keep snapping and rubbing in the butter until the pieces are about the size of a hazelnut.

In a small bowl, combine 4 tablespoons of the ice water with the vinegar and pour it over the flour mixture, leaving the ice behind. Toss to combine until the dough holds together. You want the pastry to look crumbly in the bowl and to hold together in a ball when squeezed in your hands. If a portion of the dough has come together but there is still loose butter and flour in the bottom of the bowl, remove the hydrated portion, set it aside on a work surface, and add a little more water to the bowl to bring it together.

Set out a piece of plastic wrap and transfer the dough on top. Knead once or twice to bring it together, wrap it up, and press it into a 1-inch-thick disk. By doing this now, you'll make rolling the pastry way easier later. Place the dough in the fridge for at least 2 hours or up to 2 days to rechill the butter and allow the flour to relax and hydrate.

Before rolling, remove the disk of dough from the fridge for about 5 minutes. This will allow it to warm up enough that it's easy to roll but not so much that the butter melts.

If you're making a galette, simply roll out the dough on a floured work surface according to the recipe and use

continued

If you're making a fruit pie or your recipe requires an unbaked shell, lightly dust a work surface with flour, unwrap the dough, and dust the top with a little more flour. Roll the dough out into a ¼-inch-thick circle, giving the dough a quarter turn every few rolls to help maintain a circle, keep the dough from sticking, and avoid shrinkage in the oven. You want your pastry circle to be about 3 inches wider all the way around than the top rim of your pie plate.

Roll the pastry onto your rolling pin and drape it into a pie plate. Gently press the pastry into the plate using the back of your knuckles and trim the pie dough so that it hangs about 1 inch over the edge of the plate. Tuck the overhang underneath itself to create a slightly thicker crust and press or pinch together to crimp the edge.

Transfer the unbaked shell into the fridge to chill for at least 30 minutes or up to overnight, covered in plastic, then use as directed in the recipe.

If your recipe calls for a par-baked or fully baked pie shell, use a fork to prick the bottom of the crust about a dozen times—this will allow any steam buildup to escape when the crust bakes. Preheat your oven to 400°F and set the oven rack to the bottom position.

Retrieve the pie shell from the fridge, crumple up a large square of parchment paper, press it into the shell, and fill it completely with the dried beans. You want the beans to come all the way up to the top of the pie shell so that they help hold up the sides of the pastry in place while it bakes.

Place the pie shell onto a baking sheet and bake for 18 to 20 minutes or until the edge is beginning to turn golden brown and is set. Carefully remove the parchment and beans and return the pie shell to the oven for 5 minutes if the recipe calls for a par-baked shell or 10 to 15 minutes or until golden and crisp for a fully blind-baked shell.

Par- or blind baking can be done up to 24 hours before finishing the pie.

continued

Notes on a perfect crust:

* While I prefer an all-butter pastry, it's fine to swap in cold shortening or lard.

* If you are looking to make a vegan crust, you can use vegan butter sticks or coconut oil. If opting for coconut oil, I suggest measuring it out and chilling in the freezer for 30 minutes before cutting it into the flour using a food processor. It melts at a lower temperature, making it difficult to handle.

* The science behind adding vinegar (or vodka or whatever your family recipe includes) into pastry is less than sound but, since my nana did it, I do too. Feel free to swap it out for a splash more water.

* To avoid developing too much gluten, mix and knead the dough as little as possible.

* Until it hits the heat of the oven, pastry loves being cold. If while making the pastry the butter ever feels soft or your hands get shiny, just pop the bowl in the fridge or freezer for a few minutes to rechill.

* Rest is key to allow the fat to rechill and to relax any gluten you've developed while mixing, kneading, or rolling.

* Setting the dough on the counter for 5 minutes before rolling will make it easier to roll out.

* Don't skimp on the beans (I've made this mistake more often than I care to admit). If you are blind baking, fill the shell all the way to the top so that the beans hold the bottom and sides of the pastry in place.

* Pie beans can be used over and over—just don't try to cook them for eating, as they will be super dried out.

* Baking a pie on a baking sheet is a good idea in case any butter leaks out of the pastry.

* Always bake raw pastry on the bottom rack of your oven, whether you're blind baking a shell, making a galette, or baking a fruit-filled pie. This will help keep soggy bottoms at bay and ensure that the bottom of the crust is crisp and fully cooked.

Fresh Strawberry Pie with Stable Whipped Cream

MAKES ONE 9-INCH PIE

1 batch Basic Pastry, recipe on page 213

6 cups fresh strawberries, trimmed

1 cup + 3 tablespoons granulated sugar, divided

3½ tablespoons cornstarch

½ vanilla bean, scraped and divided

1½ cups 35% whipping cream

Note:

Since this is such a simple pie, I like to splurge on a vanilla bean, but if you'd prefer to use vanilla extract, substitute 1 teaspoon of vanilla extract for the ½ vanilla bean. If you do use a bean, make sure that none of that vanilla goodness goes to waste. Add the scraped pod to your bottle of vanilla extract to give it a boost of pure vanilla flavor.

There is a diner right next to where I buy all my glasses frames that makes a mean fresh strawberry pie. A crisp crust filled to the brim with juicy strawberries, it's only made better when every inch of it is covered in a mountain of whipped cream. To mimic that whipped topping texture you only get at small-town bakeries and diners, make sure to whip your cream on medium speed as that adds air more slowly, allowing the bubbles to become stronger and therefore more stable.

Prepare the pastry and blind bake it fully. Alternatively, you can use a frozen pastry shell that you've blind baked.

Prepare the strawberries by halving or quartering any large berries, leaving smaller berries whole.

Whisk 1 cup of the sugar with the cornstarch in a medium saucepan. Add 2 cups of the strawberries and mash until juicy and a bit jammy. Stir in ½ cup of water, set over medium heat, and bring to a boil, stirring frequently until the mixture is thick and coats the back of the spoon, 3 to 5 minutes. Stir in half of the vanilla bean seeds and set the mixture aside to cool slightly.

Fold the remaining strawberries into the slightly cooled mixture and transfer to the cooled pie shell. Place the pie in the fridge for at least 3 hours or until set.

When ready to serve, whip the cream with the remaining 3 tablespoons of sugar and vanilla bean seeds on medium speed until stiff peaks form, 3 to 4 minutes. You want the whipped cream to hold its shape so it stands up on top of the pie.

Dollop, spread, or pipe the whipped cream on top of the pie, garnish with a few fresh strawberries if desired, and serve.

The pie will keep in the fridge for up to 4 days.

Cinnamon Cream Cheese & Peach Galette

MAKES ONE 10-INCH GALETTE

DINNER
PARTY
DESSERT

GREAT
GIFTING

WEEKEND
PROJECT

1 batch Basic Pastry, recipe
on page 213

½ cup brick-style cream
cheese, room temperature

2 tablespoons + ¼ cup packed
brown sugar, divided

1 teaspoon cinnamon, divided

1 teaspoon vanilla extract,
divided

1 tablespoon cornstarch

5 peaches, stones removed
and cut into 8 wedges each

1 egg

1 tablespoon milk

2 tablespoons turbinado
sugar, optional

If you've never made a pie, I suggest you start with a galette. It's a flat, free-form pie that requires no fancy shaping or crimping, and it pretty much guarantees a crisp crust, thereby making it the only pie that you can pick up and eat with your hands. As an added bonus, it's the perfect gifting pie as it doesn't even require a pie plate.

Prepare the Basic Pastry up to the galette stage.

Place your oven rack to the lowest position and preheat it to 400°F. Line a baking sheet with parchment paper.

In a medium bowl, beat the cream cheese with 2 tablespoons of the brown sugar, ½ teaspoon of the cinnamon, and ½ teaspoon of the vanilla until smooth. Set aside.

In a large bowl, stir the remaining ¼ cup of sugar and ½ teaspoon of cinnamon with the cornstarch. Add the peaches and remaining ½ teaspoon of vanilla, stir well to combine, and set aside.

On a lightly floured surface, roll the dough into a 14-inch circle and transfer it to the prepared baking sheet. Spread the cream cheese mixture over the dough, leaving about a 2-inch border, then top with the peach mixture. Fold the edges of the galette up over the fruit to form a crust.

In a small bowl, whisk together the egg and milk. Brush the mixture onto the galette crust and sprinkle with turbinado sugar.

Bake for 35 to 40 minutes or until the crust is golden brown and the fruit is tender. Cool to room temperature before serving.

Note

If the peaches at your farmer's market or grocery store aren't ripe, any other stone fruit will go beautifully with this cinnamon cream cheese filling. If using a smaller fruit such as apricots or cherries, buy enough to give you 4 to 4½ cups of sliced fruit.

Mary's Lemon Meringue Pie

MAKES ONE 9-INCH PIE

FOR THE PASTRY

1 batch Basic Pastry, recipe
   on page 213

FOR THE FILLING

1¼ cups granulated sugar

½ cup cornstarch

¼ teaspoon salt

4 egg yolks

1 tablespoon butter

½ teaspoon vanilla extract

1 lemon, zested

½ cup lemon juice

FOR THE MERINGUE

4 egg whites

¼ teaspoon salt

¼ teaspoon cream of tartar
   or lemon juice

½ cup sugar

½ teaspoon vanilla extract

They say some things skip a generation and, in my family, that is true when it comes to pastry skills. My mom hates making pie dough, but my nana, after whom I'm named, was a wizard at it and would whip up a fresh lemon meringue pie every single Friday as a follow-up to her homemade mac and cheese. While a snazzed-up version of this pie got me my spot on *MasterChef Canada*, I don't think anything beats the classic.

Prepare the pastry and blind bake it fully. Alternatively, you can use a frozen pastry shell that you've blind baked. Set aside to cool.

Keep your oven on, or preheat it to 400°F.

For the filling, whisk the sugar, cornstarch, and salt together in a medium saucepan. Whisk in 2½ cups of water and turn the heat on to medium. Bring the mixture to a boil, whisking frequently, until it is thick and glossy, 3 to 5 minutes.

Meanwhile, carefully separate four eggs and place the yolks in a heatproof bowl, saving the whites for the meringue. While whisking, slowly stream about 1 cup of the sugar mixture into the egg yolks. Go slowly so that you don't curdle or cook the yolks. Transfer the yolk mixture to the pot and cook for 1 minute, whisking constantly. Remove the pot from the heat and whisk in the butter, vanilla, lemon zest, and lemon juice. Pour the filling into the cooled crust and cover the surface directly with plastic wrap. Immediately prepare the meringue.

For the meringue, whip the egg whites, salt, and cream of tartar on medium speed until foamy. Turn the speed up to high and gradually sprinkle in the sugar, followed by the vanilla. Continue to whip just until the egg whites hold medium stiff peaks—do not over whip the egg whites or they will become weepy and watery when baked. When you lift the beaters out of the meringue, you want the tip to gently fold over itself into a soft nerve ice cream curlicue.

continued

Remove the plastic from the pie and dollop about half of the meringue on top of the filling. Spread it into an even layer so that it reaches the crust. Using a butter knife or bamboo skewer, swirl through the meringue and filling to further affix the two. Decoratively dollop or pipe the remaining meringue on top then bake the pie for 4 to 5 minutes or until the meringue is very lightly golden brown.

Allow the pie to cool completely to room temperature before chilling in the fridge for at least 4 hours before serving.

The pie will last loosely covered with a tent of aluminum foil in the fridge for up to 3 days. Do not cover it tightly or use plastic wrap, as that will lead to a weepy meringue.

Note:

Cream of tartar is an acidic by-product of wine production and helps stabilize whipped egg whites, giving you thick, glossy meringue that is easier to work with. If you do not have any on hand, another acid like lemon juice or white vinegar will work.

Black Forest Tart

MAKES ONE 10-INCH TART

DINNER
PARTY
DESSERT

WEEKEND
PROJECT

1¾ cups graham cracker crumbs

6 tablespoons cocoa powder

3 tablespoons granulated sugar

½ teaspoon kosher salt, divided

6 tablespoons melted butter

1 cup cherry jam

9 oz dark chocolate, divided

½ cup milk

2 tablespoons sugar

1½ teaspoons gelatin powder

1¼ cups 35% whipping cream, divided

2 teaspoons kirsch, optional

1 cup fresh sweet cherries

Hello, Chocolate City, USA! That's my other name for this deceptively simple tart inspired by the flavors of Black Forest cake. It is rich and dense with pops of bright cherry flavor and, despite its dainty appearance, serves a crowd.

Preheat your oven to 375°F and lightly grease a shallow pie dish or a 10-inch removable-bottom tart pan, then set on a baking sheet.

In a large bowl, stir together the graham cracker crumbs, cocoa powder, sugar, and ¼ teaspoon of salt. Add the melted butter and stir to combine. Press the mixture into the prepared pan and bake for 8 to 10 minutes or until the center is set. Set aside to cool completely to room temperature.

When cool, carefully spread the cherry jam over the bottom of the crust.

Using a large chef's or serrated knife, finely chop the chocolate. Transfer about 6 oz to a large bowl and the remaining 3 oz to a smaller bowl and set aside.

In a small saucepan or in the microwave, heat the milk and sugar together until the mixture is hot and the sugar is dissolved. Pour the milk mixture into the larger bowl of chocolate and set aside for 5 minutes to melt. Meanwhile, bloom the gelatin powder by sprinkling it over 2 tablespoons of cold tap water. When fully bloomed, add the gelatin to the chocolate and milk mixture along with the remaining ¼ teaspoon of salt and whisk well to melt the chocolate and combine. Pour in ¾ cup of cold whipping cream and, using an immersion or stand blender, blend until smooth. Give the bowl a couple of sturdy taps on the counter to remove some of the air bubbles that might have developed, then carefully pour the chocolate mixture into the crust.

Refrigerate for 4 hours to chill and set.

continued

Heat the remaining ½ cup of cream in a small saucepan or in the microwave until very hot then pour it over the remaining 3 oz of chocolate. Allow it to sit for 10 minutes to melt the chocolate, then add the kirsch and whisk until the mixture is smooth. Allow the ganache to cool until it is a thick and pourable consistency, then carefully pour on top of the chilled tart.

Place in the fridge for at least another hour to firm up, then decorate with fresh cherries and serve.

This tart will keep covered in your fridge for up to 1 week.

Note:

Blooming gelatin is the process of hydrating powdered gelatin crystals or softening gelatin sheets in cold water before adding to a warm liquid to dissolve. If you were to just add dry gelatin to a hot liquid, it would not hydrate, leaving your dessert unset and grainy.

Blackberry Apple Cream Cheese Cobbler

SERVES 6 TO 8

1 pint blackberries

4 green apples, peeled and diced

½ cup packed brown sugar

½ teaspoon ground ginger

¼ teaspoon cinnamon

1 tablespoon cornstarch

1 orange, zested and juiced

1½ cups all-purpose flour

2 tablespoons sugar

2 teaspoons baking powder

½ teaspoon kosher salt

½ cup butter, cold and cut into pats

½ cup brick-style cream cheese, cold and cut into pats

¾ cup buttermilk

1 teaspoon vanilla extract

Vanilla ice cream, for serving

Cobblers, crumbles, crisps, bettys, buckles, and grunts are all delish and versatile desserts that go from oven to table in the same dish. In my opinion, cobblers reign supreme by combining fluffy drop biscuits with sweet, stewy fruit, but any dessert that can double as breakfast is A++ in my books.

Preheat your oven to 375°F and lightly grease a large cast-iron skillet or casserole dish with nonstick cooking spray or room-temperature butter.

In a large bowl, gently mix the blackberries, diced apples, brown sugar, ginger, cinnamon, and cornstarch until well combined. Stir in the orange zest and juice and transfer the fruit and any accumulated juices to the prepared skillet.

In the same bowl, combine the flour, sugar, baking powder, and salt. Toss in the pats of butter and cream cheese and, using a pastry cutter or your fingers, cut or snap them in until the pats are about the size of a chickpea. Using a wooden spoon or spatula, make a well in the middle of the dry ingredients. Pour in the buttermilk and vanilla and stir just until combined.

Using two large spoons or a spring-loaded ice cream scoop, drop the biscuit mixture overtop of the fruit. Place the skillet cobbler onto a baking sheet and bake for 45 to 50 minutes or until the fruit is tender and the biscuits are golden on top and springy to the touch.

Allow the cobbler to cool for at least 15 minutes before serving warm with a scoop of ice cream.

Note:

Baking recipes typically call for green apples due to their tart flavor and crisp texture. Their tartness acts to balance the sweetness of sugar, and their firmness holds up to the heat of the oven, keeping some crisp apple texture in the end result. If you don't mind a more tender, pudding-y fruit filling, a softer, sweeter apple such as McIntosh will also work.

Cannoli Bougatsa

SERVES 6 TO 8

½ cup sugar

1 tablespoon cornstarch

½ teaspoon cinnamon

¼ teaspoon kosher salt

1 cup milk

1 cup ricotta

3 egg yolks

1 egg

2 teaspoons vanilla extract
  or 1 vanilla bean, scraped

1 orange, zested

12 phyllo sheets

½ cup unsalted melted butter

1½ oz chopped dark chocolate
  or chocolate chips

¼ cup chopped pistachios

Cinnamon and icing sugar,
  for dusting

If you're in the market for a crispy golden-brown dessert with a sweet, creamy filling, Italian and Greek pastries are for you! With this recipe, a creamy cannoli-inspired ricotta filling takes the place of traditional pastry cream in this classic Greek dessert, bringing two of my favorite pastries together at last.

Preheat your oven to 325°F and set out a 9-inch high-sided cake pan or deep-dish pie plate.

In a large bowl, whisk together the sugar, cornstarch, cinnamon, and salt until well combined. Whisk in the milk followed by the ricotta, egg yolks, whole egg, vanilla, and orange zest. Set aside.

Lay out the phyllo sheets and lightly brush the cake pan with melted butter. Lay a sheet of phyllo into the pan and press it across the bottom and up the sides. Brush with 1 to 2 teaspoons of melted butter and place another piece of phyllo on top, perpendicular to the first. Brush with 1 to 2 teaspoons of butter and continue this layering with four more sheets of phyllo.

Brush the remaining sheets of phyllo with butter, crumple each up into a loose ball, and place on top of the phyllo base in a single layer. Fold any overhanging phyllo up and crumple it into the pan, then pour in the ricotta mixture. Scatter the chocolate and pistachios overtop.

Bake for 40 to 45 minutes or until golden brown and crisp.

Allow the cannoli bougatsa to cool slightly or fully to room temperature before slicing and serving dusted with cinnamon and icing sugar, if desired.

Note:

Phyllo gets a reputation for being difficult to work with, but I disagree. Yes, it tears easily and the raw sheets of dough can dry out faster than other pastries, but all of those rips and slightly crispy bits add to the overall texture of the end result. If one layer rips or has a dry edge, butter and another layer of pastry will cover it up.

Dulce de Leche Pavlova

SERVES 8

1 can sweetened condensed
  milk or store-bought dulce
  de leche

1¼ cups pecans

1¼ cups sugar, divided

1 teaspoon cornstarch

5 egg whites

½ teaspoon kosher salt

¼ teaspoon cream of tartar,
  lemon juice, or white vinegar

1½ teaspoons vanilla extract,
  divided

2 cups 35% whipping cream

Flaky sea salt, optional

Note:

When making meringue,
always use a metal, glass, or
ceramic bowl. Plastic tends
to hold onto fat and oil,
which will lead to a weepy
meringue. To be extra sure
your meringue will whip up
in a fat-free environment,
use a clean piece of paper
towel to wipe down the bowl
and beaters just before
whipping the egg whites.

Pavlova is a delicate and light dessert but, like the vocation of its namesake, it's stronger than you might think. Obviously, you shouldn't toss it around or drop it on purpose, but if it does break, just take a page out of British cookery books and call it an Eton Mess.

To make dulce de leche, remove the label from the can of sweetened condensed milk, but keep the can closed, and set it in a saucepan. (If you're using store-bought dulce de leche, you can skip this step.) Cover the can with at least 1 inch of water and bring to a boil over medium-high heat. Reduce the heat to low, cover with a lid, and allow it to gently simmer for 2½ hours, checking on the water level every 20 to 30 minutes and topping it up if needed to keep the can submerged. Remove the pan from the heat and leave the can in the water to cool to room temperature.

Preheat your oven to 250°F and line two baking sheets with parchment paper.

In a small pan over medium heat, toast the pecans, stirring frequently, until they smell nutty, 1 to 2 minutes. Set aside to cool then coarsely chop half of the pecans. Finely chop the remaining pecans and set aside.

In a small bowl, stir together 1 cup of the sugar and the cornstarch and set aside.

Place the egg whites, salt, and cream of tartar in a large bowl (see note) and whip on high until soft, foamy peaks form, about 30 seconds. With the mixer running, slowly sprinkle in the sugar mixture and continue to whip until the meringue is glossy and holds stiff peaks when the beaters are lifted out of the mixture, about 3 minutes. Whip in 1 teaspoon of the vanilla.

Using a spatula or metal spoon, gently fold in the finely chopped pecans. Divide the meringue between the two prepared baking sheets and spread each into an 8-inch circle.

continued

Bake the meringues for 1 hour and 15 minutes, then turn the oven off and allow them to cool in the oven for at least 30 minutes or until the oven is fully cool.

When the meringues are cool, make the whipped cream by beating the whipping cream with the remaining ¼ cup of sugar and the remaining ½ teaspoon of vanilla on medium speed until stiff peaks form.

To assemble, place one of the meringues on a cake pedestal or plate and top with half of the whipped cream. Drizzle or dollop over some dulce de leche and scatter on half of the coarsely chopped pecans. Repeat these layers, using as much dulce de leche as you'd like. To cut the sweetness, sprinkle a pinch of flaky sea salt on top just before serving.

Spiced Apple Cheesecake

MAKES ONE 9-INCH CHEESECAKE

FOR THE CHEESECAKE

7 oz crispy spice cookies, such
as Biscoff or gingersnaps

1 tablespoon all-purpose flour

¼ teaspoon kosher salt

6 tablespoons melted butter

1¼ cups sugar, divided

3 tablespoons cornstarch

½ teaspoon cinnamon

3 cups brick-style cream
cheese, room temperature

3 eggs

2 teaspoons vanilla extract

⅔ cup 35% whipping cream

**FOR THE SPICED APPLE
TOPPING**

4 green apples, peeled
and cored

½ lemon

1 tablespoon butter

1 tablespoon apple brandy,
optional

¼ cup packed brown sugar

1–2 teaspoons cinnamon

¼ teaspoon kosher salt

I'm not gonna lie, classic baked cheesecakes can be finicky, and making a perfect one without any cracks is not the easiest thing in the world. Sure, there are things you can do like adding a bit of cornstarch to the batter, not overbeating the eggs, and using a water bath to protect the delicate custard from the direct heat of the oven, but sometimes, even after following every precaution, your cheesecake splits. But have no fear! All is well! That's what the spiced apple topping is for. Just pile it on, and no one will be any the wiser.

Preheat your oven to 350°F, grease a 9-inch springform pan with nonstick cooking spray, and wrap the outside of the pan with aluminum foil. Set inside a larger baking pan and put a kettle on to boil.

For the cheesecake, in a food processor, blitz the cookies into fine crumbs. Add the flour, salt, and melted butter and pulse to combine. Press into the bottom of the prepared pan and bake for 8 minutes. Remove from the oven and allow the crust to cool.

Meanwhile, whisk together ½ cup of sugar with the cornstarch and cinnamon in a large bowl or the bowl of a stand mixer. Add 1 cup of cream cheese and beat on medium speed until well combined, about 1 minute. Add the remaining cream cheese and sugar and beat on medium speed until creamy, 1 to 2 minutes. Scrape down the bowl and beat in the eggs, one at a time, on medium speed followed by the vanilla. Add the cream and continue to beat just until completely smooth, 1 to 2 minutes, scraping the bowl as needed.

Pour the filling onto the cooled crust. Pour the hot boiled water into the larger pan until it comes about halfway up the side of the springform pan to create a water bath. Carefully transfer to the oven and bake for 1 hour to 1 hour 15 minutes or until the edge of the cheesecake is set but the center still has a wobble.

Remove the cheesecake from the water bath and allow it to cool completely to room temperature. Cover and transfer to the fridge to chill for at least 4 hours or up to 4 days.

continued

For the topping, slice the apples into thin wedges and squeeze the lemon juice over them, tossing to coat. Melt the butter in a large sauté pan or skillet over medium heat then add the apples. Cook, stirring frequently, until slightly softened, 2 to 4 minutes. Deglaze the pan with the brandy, if using, and allow it to simmer for 30 seconds to 1 minute, until almost all the liquid has evaporated. Add the sugar, cinnamon, and salt and continue to cook until sticky and the apples are quite soft but still holding their shape, 1 to 2 minutes. Remove from the heat to cool slightly.

The topping can be served warm on top of slices of chilled cheesecake or cooled to room temperature and spooned over the whole cheesecake and chilled in the fridge until ready to serve.

Note:

Whenever cutting a dense dessert like a cream pie, fudgy brownies, or cheesecake, warm your knife under hot water and dry it before slicing, and wipe the knife between each cut. This ensures clean and even edges on each slice.

Grilled Stone-Fruit Melba

SERVES 4

6 stone fruits, such as plums,
  peaches, nectarines,
  or apricots

1 tablespoon olive oil

1 cup raspberries, fresh or
  frozen and thawed

1 tablespoon icing sugar

1 tablespoon orange liqueur

1 cup vanilla Greek yogurt

1–2 tablespoons honey

8 gingersnaps or spice cookies,
  roughly crumbled

This is the perfect last-minute summer dessert. By grilling the stone fruit, you add a little bit of welcome bitterness to this sweet, low-prep showstopper. While it's traditionally made with peaches, I say go with whatever looks best for your summery melba.

Heat your grill to medium-high.

Cut the stone fruits in half and remove the pits. If the pits don't easily come out, use a small teaspoon or melon baller to scoop them out. Drizzle the cut sides of the fruits with the oil and place on the grill, cut side down, for 2 to 4 minutes or until char marks appear. Set aside.

Meanwhile, puree the raspberries, icing sugar, and orange liqueur together using an immersion blender or a small smoothie blender. For a smooth sauce, strain through a fine-mesh sieve to remove the raspberry seeds.

To serve, divide the yogurt into four shallow bowls and top with the raspberry puree and grilled stone fruit. Drizzle with honey and scatter with the crumbled cookies.

Note:

Being a slow ice cream eater, I prefer serving this dessert with Greek yogurt on warm summer nights but, if you'd prefer to keep it a little more classic, swap the yogurt for vanilla ice cream.

Almond Cherry Brownie Pudding

SERVES 8

4 eggs

1 cup granulated sugar

¾ cup packed brown sugar

½ teaspoon kosher salt

2 teaspoons vanilla extract

1 teaspoon almond extract

1 tablespoon almond liqueur, optional

¾ cup cocoa powder

½ cup all-purpose flour

1 cup unsalted butter, melted and cooled

½ cup almond butter

1 cup pitted fresh or frozen, thawed cherries

Vanilla or cherry ice cream, for serving

Toasted slivered almonds, optional

Note:

Baked goods without chemical leaveners still require something to provide some lift as they bake in the oven. In this dessert and in recipes for chiffon or angel food cakes, whipped eggs provide the levity required for a light bake with a tender crumb.

Over the pandemic, the thing I continually craved was not some fancy ten-course extravaganza at a snazzy restaurant but rather an everyday meal of apps and 'zerts from a certain Canadian chain. Keep your truffles and foams; give me a platter of baked spinach dip and deep-fried pita triangles with a chocolate brownie lava cake for dessert! While there's no real substitute for the specific spinach dip experience I crave, this almond cherry brownie pudding is definitely an improvement on the original and is a cinch to whip up.

Preheat your oven to 325°F and put a kettle on to boil. Lightly grease a large cast-iron skillet or 2-quart shallow casserole dish with nonstick cooking spray and set inside a larger baking pan, such as a roasting pan.

In a large bowl or the bowl of a stand mixer fitted with the whisk attachment, beat the eggs, granulated sugar, brown sugar, and salt together on high speed for 5 to 7 minutes until very light and fluffy and tripled in volume. Beat in the vanilla extract, almond extract, and almond liqueur and set aside.

In a separate bowl, sift the cocoa powder and flour together then whisk well. Add to the egg and sugar mixture and gently fold just to combine. Stir in the butter and transfer to the prepared skillet. Drizzle the almond butter overtop and scatter in the cherries.

Carefully pour the boiled water into the large pan so that it comes about halfway up the side of the skillet, then transfer to the oven. Bake for 50 to 55 minutes or until the top is crisp looking and matte. The pudding should still wobble quite a bit.

Remove the skillet pudding from the water bath and set aside to cool slightly. Serve the pudding in bowls topped with a scoop of ice cream and slivered almonds.

Basics

BANG FOR
YOUR BUCK

FOOD
WASTE

GET
AHEAD

ONE
POT-ISH

Chicken Stock

MAKES 4 QUARTS

2½–3 lb chicken bones
   or carcasses

4 stalks celery

3 carrots

2 yellow onions

1 head garlic

1 handful parsley stalks

6 sprigs thyme

3 bay leaves

1½ teaspoons black
   peppercorns

1 tablespoon kosher salt

Stock is the perfect food scrap saver and it can be made with fresh, roasted, or frozen chicken bones or carcasses. It sounds maybe a bit morbid, but I save the carcasses of roasted chickens and the backbones of spatchcocked chickens in a large freezer bag for up to three months. Anytime carrots, onions, or celery are starting to look a little sad in my veg drawer, I add them to the bag along with the stems of parsley and other herbs. That way, all I have to do is dump the contents into a big pot, cover them with water, and let them simmer away.

Place the chicken bones or carcasses into a large stock pot.

Chop the celery and carrots into large chunks and add them to the pot. Leave the onions and garlic unpeeled, cut them in half, and place in the pot along with the parsley stalks, thyme, bay leaves, peppercorns, and salt. Pour in 5 quarts of water, adding more if the veg and chicken bones are not fully covered.

Place the pot over high heat, bring to a boil, then immediately reduce the heat to low to maintain a low simmer. Simmer the stock for at least 4 hours, occasionally skimming any frothy foam that floats to the surface.

When the stock is flavorful and the chicken bones break apart easily, scoop out as much of the chicken and veg as possible then strain the stock through a fine-mesh sieve. Allow the stock to cool to room temperature before transferring to resealable containers and storing in the fridge for up to 1 week or in the freezer for up to 3 months.

Note:

In addition to carrots, celery, and onion, things like fennel, leeks, shallots, and parsnips are great added to the stock. Just steer clear of any veg that bleeds color like beets or anything from the cabbage family like broccoli, as that will make your stock a bit, well, farty.

Vegetable Broth

MAKES 4 QUARTS

1 tablespoon olive oil

5 stalks celery

5 carrots

1 bulb fennel

1 leek

2 yellow onions

1 head garlic

1 handful parsley stalks

6 sprigs thyme

2 sprigs rosemary

3 bay leaves

1½ teaspoons black peppercorns

1 tablespoon kosher salt

2–4 tablespoons nutritional yeast, optional

BANG FOR YOUR BUCK

FOOD WASTE

GET HEAD

ONE POT-ISH

Similar to chicken stock, vegetable broth is an easy way to use up food scraps and get every last ounce of flavor from your veg. Personally, I'm not a huge fan of tomato-y vegetable broth, but if you like that rich, slightly sweet flavor of tomato, add tomato scraps to the freezer bag and stir a couple of teaspoons of tomato paste into the pot when simmering the broth.

Place a large stock pot over medium-high heat. Add the oil.

Chop the celery, carrots, fennel, and leek into large chunks, rinse the leek to remove any sand trapped between the layers, and add to the pot. Leave the onions and head of garlic unpeeled, cut them in half, and place in the pot along with the parsley stalks, thyme, rosemary, bay leaves, peppercorns, and salt.

Pour in 5 quarts of water and bring to a boil then immediately reduce the heat to low. Stir in the nutritional yeast and simmer the broth for at least 1½ hours or until the broth is rich in flavor.

Scoop out as much veg as possible then strain the broth through a fine-mesh sieve. Allow the broth to cool to room temperature before transferring to resealable containers and storing in the fridge for up to 1 week or in the freezer for up to 3 months.

Note:

Nutritional yeast is deactivated baker's or brewer's yeast. It contains protein and fiber and is often fortified with additional vitamins and nutrients. Nutty and super savory, it is often used in vegan or vegetarian cooking to impart an almost Parmesan cheesy flavor. Use it in vegan cheese sauces, mashed potatoes, or even sprinkled over popcorn.

FAST
FLAVOR

FOOD
WASTE

GET
AHEAD

ONE
POT-ISH

My Go-To Pesto

MAKES 1½ CUPS

1 cup loosely packed fresh basil

½ cup loosely packed fresh parsley

½ cup loosely packed arugula or baby spinach

¼ cup finely ground Parmigiano-Reggiano cheese

¼ cup pine nuts

2 garlic cloves, peeled and smashed

½ lemon, zested and juiced

6 tablespoons extra virgin olive oil, plus more if desired

Kosher salt

Freshly ground black pepper

Pesto is one of my favorite speedy flavor shortcuts. I like to whisk it into eggs before scrambling, add it to mayo for an extra flavor boost on any sandwich, stir it into canned crushed tomatoes for an easy tomato sauce, spread it onto a grilled cheese sandwich because why not, mash it into butter to serve with steak, or simply mix it with pasta and a spoonful of pasta water for a quick and herby dinner.

Add the basil, parsley, arugula, Parmigiano-Reggiano, pine nuts, and garlic to the bowl of a food processor, a stand blender, or a mortar and pestle. Pulse or bash to roughly chop and combine. Add the lemon zest, lemon juice, and oil and blend until the pesto reaches your desired consistency, adding more oil if needed. Personally, I like a thicker pesto with some texture. If needed, I can always add more oil later. Season with salt and pepper, to taste.

Transfer the pesto to a resealable container or jar and store in the fridge for up to 2 weeks. To help seal in flavor, I like to drizzle a little extra oil on top to cover the surface of the pesto.

Use on and in anything that could use a bright, garlicky, herby kick.

Note:

Pesto can be made with any fine herbs you have in your crisper and is a great way to extend their shelf life. In addition to using different herbs, you can use any hard cheese in place of the Parmigiano-Reggiano and any nuts in place of the pine nuts. In my mind, there's no wrong answer when it comes to pesto, so just find the flavors that work for you.

No-Yeast Flatbread

MAKES 6

FAST
FLAVOR

ONE
POT-ISH

PANTRY
STAPLE

1¾–2 cups all-purpose flour

1 teaspoon baking powder

¾ teaspoon kosher salt

⅔ cup warm water

3 tablespoons olive oil

Ever open your cupboard with a carby craving only to find that you're out of bread? This quick no-yeast flatbread is here to save the day. See the photo on page 164 for Pizza Today/Pizza Tomorrow.

In a large bowl, stir 1¾ cups of flour with the baking powder and salt until well combined. Make a well in the center, add the warm water and oil, and stir into a shaggy dough, adding more flour if the dough is sticky.

Dust a work surface well with extra flour and turn out the dough. Knead the dough for about 1 minute until smooth then set aside under a clean dish towel to rest for 20 minutes.

Once rested, divide the dough into six pieces and roll each out on a floured work surface into a ¼-inch-thick oval.

Heat a large skillet over medium-high heat. Cook the flatbreads, one at a time, for about 2 minutes per side or until golden and springy.

Serve warm or allow to cool to room temperature. Store any leftover flatbreads in a resealable bag for up to 4 days.

Note:

To make whole wheat flatbreads, substitute whole wheat flour for the all-purpose flour. Since whole wheat flour absorbs more liquid than all-purpose flour, you will need to add a few more tablespoons of water when bringing the dough together.

Basic Polenta

SERVES 4

4 cups water, broth, or stock

2 garlic cloves, finely grated

Kosher salt

Freshly ground black pepper

1 cup cornmeal

2 tablespoons butter

The mashed potatoes of the corn world, polenta is quicker and, while this is difficult for me to admit as a lifelong potato lover, arguably more versatile than its spud-based counterpart. Also, it's a great use-it-up base for odds and ends hanging around your fridge like olive tapenade, pesto, nubs of cheese, or chilis in oil. See the photo on page 89 for Creamy Polenta with Greens, Tomatoes & Cheese.

In a medium pot with a tight-fitting lid, bring the water to a boil over high heat.

Add the garlic, ½ teaspoon of salt, and ¼ teaspoon of pepper, then slowly whisk in the cornmeal. Stir constantly until the mixture starts to thicken, about 15 seconds. Cover, reduce the heat to low, and allow it to simmer until thickened, about 20 minutes, stirring every 5 minutes or so.

Remove the polenta from the heat, whisk in the butter as well as any mix-ins such as grated cheese or chopped herbs, and season to taste with more salt and pepper, if needed.

Serve warm in shallow bowls or transfer to a lightly greased 9-inch square baking pan and place in the fridge to firm up. Once firm, the polenta can be sliced and fried in a little butter or oil until crisp.

Note:

Many polenta recipes call for it to be cooked for at least 1 hour. Personally, I don't agree and see little to no difference in the end result. That being said, a longer cooking time doesn't negatively impact the flavor or texture of the polenta.

Thank You!

While in the past I've started with thank yous to those closest to me, this time I'm going to start by saying that from the get-go, this book has been inspired by you!

Over the years, hearing from you and getting to see the recipes that I write come to be some of your family favorites fills me with more joy than I could ever express. So, thank you! Thank you for inviting me into your home through my books and cooking shows, for being as excited as I am about food, for being curious about cooking, and for sharing your creations with the people you love.

To Aaron, it's almost embarrassing how great I think you are. Thank you for digging into every recipe I've ever written, for doing more than your fair share of dishes, and for putting up with my "office" moving to a different part of the house every couple of weeks. Truly, none of this would be possible without you.

Mom, I'm thrilled to be a conduit between your hilariousness and the world. Thank you for your constant support and encouragement, even when it takes the form of endless questions about the recipe we're eating for dinner.

To Jenna and Lauren, thank you for lending your wonderful artistry to this book and for bringing the recipes to life. The energy and excitement that you shared with me while we shot these recipes finally made this book feel real, and that means more than I can say.

To my glorious team at Appetite by Random House, thank you for your unending support, expertise, and exuberance about all things food and all things cookbook! Robert and Zoe, I can't wait to keep making delish little cookbook babies with you both! And Jen, I'm beyond thrilled to have your unmatched eye for design on these pages.

Thank you to Marisa for testing every recipe that needed an extra set of eyes, Lindsay for loudly proclaiming to anyone who gives even the slightest sign of interest, "She's my cousin!," Richelle for literally keeping my brain from exploding, and Allison for being a fierce friend and for making me feel as if I'm on the right track, even when I'm spiraling. Thank you to my friends at The Food Group for access to your glorious color-coded prop room that inspired me to have "What Dreams Are Made Of" by my girl Hilary Duff stuck in my head for three weeks straight. Finally, to a man I've never met, thank you to Mike Schur for making the television shows that provided the background soundtrack for the writing of this book.

Index

A

almond butter: Almond Cherry Brownie Pudding, 240

almonds
Lemon Almond Blueberry Muffins, 24
Pan-Fried Halloumi with Greens & Romesco, 81
Whatever You Like Slice & Bake Cookies, 195–96

anchovies
Pantry Puttanesca, 97
Romaine & Endive Salad with Anchovy Lemon Dressing & Crispy Breadcrumbs, 59

apples
Apple Cinnamon Biscuit Buns, 31–32
Blackberry Apple Cream Cheese Cobbler, 228
Cider Pork Tenderloin with Autumn Veg, 175
Curried Lentil Stuffed Squash, 82
Roasted Sausage Sheet Pan Dinner, 171
Spiced Apple Cheesecake, 235–36

arugula. *See* greens

avocado
Chipotle Chicken Soup, 139
Crispy Coconut Fish Tacos, 119–20
Green Couscous Salad, 55

B

bacon
Bacon-Wrapped Meatloaf, 179–80
BLT Chicken, 150
Green Eggs sans Ham (variation), 20
Roast Beef Bourguignon, 185–86

Balsamic Grilled Radicchio & Pears, 73

Basic Pastry, 213–17

Basic Polenta, 248

basil. *See also* herbs
Balsamic Grilled Radicchio & Pears, 73
Caprese Baked Rigatoni alla Vodka, 98
My Go-To Pesto, 246

beans. *See also* chickpeas
Bistro Salad, 61–62
Black Bean Chipotle Veggie Burger, 48–49
Chipotle Breakfast Burritos, 12
Chipotle Chicken Soup, 139
Lemony Shrimp with White Beans & Garlic Toast, 125
Stewed White Beans with Greens & Chili, 84

beef, 7–8
Bacon-Wrapped Meatloaf, 179–80
French Onion Pot Roast with Gruyère Potatoes, 177–78

Reverse-Sear Steak with Chimichurri, 183
Roast Beef Bourguignon, 185–86
beer
Brine & Bake Pork Chops, 172
Irish Onion Soup, 41
berries
Blackberry Apple Cream Cheese Cobbler, 228
Fresh Strawberry Pie with Stable Whipped
Cream, 219
Grilled Stone-Fruit Melba, 239
Lemon Almond Blueberry Muffins, 24
Oat Crepes with Sweet Mascarpone &
Blackberries, 33–34
Raspberry Cheesecake Blondies, 197–98
Soft Fruit Freezer Compote, 28
Bistro Salad, 61–62
Black Forest Tart, 225–26
BLT Chicken, 150
breads (as ingredient). *See also* sandwiches
and burgers; tortillas
Bacon-Wrapped Meatloaf, 179–80
BLT Chicken, 150
Chocolate Hazelnut Croissant French Toast
Bake, 27
Irish Onion Soup, 41
Lemony Shrimp with White Beans & Garlic
Toast, 125
Pan con Tomate, 38
Roasted Garlic Bread Chicken Thighs, 149
Roasted Mushrooms with Blue Cheese
Rosemary Crumb, 77
Romaine & Endive Salad with Anchovy
Lemon Dressing & Crispy Breadcrumbs, 59
Stewed White Beans with Greens & Chili, 84
breakfast and brunch dishes, 12–34
Brine & Bake Pork Chops, 172
broccoli
Green Veg Gratin, 78
Sheet Pan Sunday Roast (variation), 159–60
Buffalo Roasted Cauliflower & Chickpea Pitas
with Blue Cheese Slaw, 46–47
butter, 7

buttermilk
Apple Cinnamon Biscuit Buns, 31–32
Blackberry Apple Cream Cheese Cobbler, 228
French Onion Pot Roast with Gruyère Potatoes,
177–78
Herbed Blinis a.k.a. Savory Pancakes, 15

C
cabbage
Crispy Coconut Fish Tacos, 119–20
Roasted Sausage Sheet Pan Dinner, 171
cakes and loaves
Chocolate Peanut Butter Cake with Cornflake
Crunch, 211–12
Coconut Loaf with Chocolate Hazelnut Glaze,
203
Lemon Cornmeal Olive Oil Cake, 205–6
Marble Zucchini Loaf with Chocolate
Cinnamon Streusel, 200–201
Spiced Apple Cheesecake, 235–36
Tiramisu Cupcakes, 207–8
Cannoli Bougatsa, 231
Caprese Baked Rigatoni alla Vodka, 98
Caramelized Shallots with Sherry Vinegar &
Pistachios, 69
carrots. *See also* vegetables
Seared Carrot Ginger Salmon, 126
Sheet Pan Sunday Roast, 159–60
cashews: Quick Coconut Butter Tofu with
Chickpeas, 87
cauliflower: Buffalo Roasted Cauliflower &
Chickpea Pitas with Blue Cheese Slaw,
46–47
celery. *See* vegetables
cheese. *See also specific types of cheese (below)*
Baked Fish Butty, 114–15
Caprese Baked Rigatoni alla Vodka, 98
Chipotle Breakfast Burritos, 12
Creamy Polenta with Greens, Tomatoes &
Cheese, 88
French Onion Pot Roast with Gruyère Potatoes,
177–78

Green Veg Gratin, 78

Lemony Shrimp with White Beans & Garlic
Toast, 125

Mushroom & Pesto Skillet Lasagna, 103–4

Pan-Fried Halloumi with Greens & Romesco,
81

Romaine & Endive Salad with Anchovy
Lemon Dressing & Crispy Breadcrumbs, 59

cheese, blue
Buffalo Roasted Cauliflower & Chickpea Pitas
with Blue Cheese Slaw, 46–47

Roasted Mushrooms with Blue Cheese
Rosemary Crumb, 77

cheese, cheddar
Crispy Mini Rösti, 19

Irish Onion Soup, 41

cheese, cream
Apple Cinnamon Biscuit Buns, 31–32

Blackberry Apple Cream Cheese Cobbler,
228

Cinnamon Cream Cheese & Peach Galette,
221

Raspberry Cheesecake Blondies, 197–98

Spiced Apple Cheesecake, 235–36

Tiramisu Cupcakes (variation), 207–8

cheese, feta
Creamed Corn Baked Feta, 66

Creamy Harissa Lamb Meatballs, 167–68

Curried Lentil Stuffed Squash, 82

Fried Feta Salad with Honey & Herbs, 56

Green Couscous Salad, 55

Mediterranean Salmon, 133

Red Pepper Hummus Tartines, 23

Sheet Pan Souvlaki, 143–44

Smoky Harissa Eggplant with Herby Feta Oil
& Pine Nuts, 74

cheese, goat
Balsamic Grilled Radicchio & Pears, 73

Fresh & Grilled Ratatouille with Provençal
Chicken, 153–54

Pizza Today/Pizza Tomorrow, 165–66

Stewed White Beans with Greens & Chili, 84

cheese, mascarpone
Oat Crepes with Sweet Mascarpone &
Blackberries, 33–34

Tiramisu Cupcakes, 207–8

cheese, Parmesan. *See also* cheese
Brine & Bake Pork Chops, 172

Chick Parm Meatballs, 145–46

Creamy Spaghetti al Limone, 94

Crispy Garlic Parmesan Potatoes with
Roasted Garlic Mayo, 51

Eggplant Parmesan, 63–64

My Go-To Pesto, 246

Parmesan Zucchini with Crispy Chickpeas
& Tahini Ricotta, 70

Roasted Garlic Bread Chicken Thighs, 149

Smoked Fish Brandade, 121–22

cheese, ricotta
Cannoli Bougatsa, 231

Lemon Cornmeal Olive Oil Cake, 205–6

Parmesan Zucchini with Crispy Chickpeas &
Tahini Ricotta, 70

Spicy Sausage Pasta with Rapini & Herbed
Ricotta, 109–10

cherries
Almond Cherry Brownie Pudding, 240

Black Forest Tart, 225–26

chicken and turkey
BLT Chicken, 150

Chicken Noodle Roast Chicken, 155–56

Chicken Stock, 244

Chick Parm Meatballs, 145–46

Chipotle Chicken Soup, 139

Creamy Harissa Lamb Meatballs (variation),
167–68

Fresh & Grilled Ratatouille with Provençal
Chicken, 153–54

Lemony Piccata (variation), 129

Roasted Garlic Bread Chicken Thighs, 149

Satay Chicken Wings with Peanut Sauce,
137–38

Sheet Pan Souvlaki, 143–44

Sheet Pan Sunday Roast, 159–60

chickpeas
> Buffalo Roasted Cauliflower & Chickpea Pitas with Blue Cheese Slaw, 46–47
> Parmesan Zucchini with Crispy Chickpeas & Tahini Ricotta, 70
> Quick Coconut Butter Tofu with Chickpeas, 87
> Red Pepper Hummus Tartines, 23

chili peppers. *See* peppers, chili

chocolate
> Almond Cherry Brownie Pudding, 240
> Black Forest Tart, 225–26
> Cannoli Bougatsa, 231
> Chocolate Hazelnut Croissant French Toast Bake, 27
> Chocolate Peanut Butter Cake with Cornflake Crunch, 211–12
> Coconut Loaf with Chocolate Hazelnut Glaze, 203
> My Dream Chocolate Chip Cookie, 190
> Whatever You Like Slice & Bake Cookies, 195–96

Cider Pork Tenderloin with Autumn Veg, 175

cilantro
> Chipotle Chicken Soup, 139
> Crispy Coconut Fish Tacos, 119–20
> Green Ginger Miso Soup, 42
> Mango Salad, 138
> Reverse-Sear Steak with Chimichurri, 183
> Satay Chicken Wings with Peanut Sauce, 137–38
> Spicy Roasted Sweet Potatoes, 52

cinnamon
> Apple Cinnamon Biscuit Buns, 31–32
> Cinnamon Cream Cheese & Peach Galette, 221
> Marble Zucchini Loaf with Chocolate Cinnamon Streusel, 200–201

coconut
> Coconut Loaf with Chocolate Hazelnut Glaze, 203
> Crispy Coconut Fish Tacos, 119–20

coconut milk
> Quick Coconut Butter Tofu with Chickpeas, 87
> Satay Chicken Wings with Peanut Sauce, 137–38

coffee
> Chocolate Peanut Butter Cake with Cornflake Crunch, 211–12
> Tiramisu Cupcakes, 207–8
> Whatever You Like Slice & Bake Cookies, 195–96

cookies and bars
> Ginger Molasses Cookies, 191
> My Dream Chocolate Chip Cookie, 190
> Raspberry Cheesecake Blondies, 197–98
> Whatever You Like Slice & Bake Cookies, 195–96

corn
> Chipotle Chicken Soup, 139
> Creamed Corn Baked Feta, 66
> Miso Butter Corn Pasta, 101–2

cornmeal and polenta
> Basic Polenta, 248
> Creamy Polenta with Greens, Tomatoes & Cheese, 88
> French Onion Pot Roast with Gruyère Potatoes (variation), 177–78
> Lemon Cornmeal Olive Oil Cake, 205–6

couscous
> Chicken Noodle Roast Chicken, 155–56
> Green Couscous Salad, 55

cream. *See also* milk
> Black Forest Tart, 225–26
> Caprese Baked Rigatoni alla Vodka, 98
> Chocolate Peanut Butter Cake with Cornflake Crunch, 211–12
> Creamy Lobster Gnocchi, 107–8
> Creamy Spaghetti al Limone, 94
> Dulce de Leche Pavlova, 233–34
> French Onion Pot Roast with Gruyère Potatoes, 177–78
> Fresh Strawberry Pie with Stable Whipped Cream, 219

Green Veg Gratin, 78

Lemon Cornmeal Olive Oil Cake, 205–6

Smoked Fish Brandade, 121–22

Spiced Apple Cheesecake, 235–36

Tiramisu Cupcakes, 207–8

Creamed Corn Baked Feta, 66

cucumber

Green Couscous Salad, 55

Mediterranean Salmon, 133

Seared Carrot Ginger Salmon, 126

Tzatziki, 144

Curried Lentil Stuffed Squash, 82

D

dairy products, 9. *See also specific items*

Dulce de Leche Pavlova, 233–34

E

eggplant

Eggplant Parmesan, 63–64

Fresh & Grilled Ratatouille with Provençal
    Chicken, 153–54

Smoky Harissa Eggplant with Herby Feta Oil
    & Pine Nuts, 74

eggs, 9

Bistro Salad, 61–62

Chipotle Breakfast Burritos, 12

Chocolate Hazelnut Croissant French Toast
    Bake, 27

Creamy Spaghetti al Limone, 94

Dulce de Leche Pavlova, 233–34

Green Eggs sans Ham, 20

Mary's Lemon Meringue Pie, 223–24

Red Pepper Hummus Tartines, 23

endive (Belgian): Romaine & Endive Salad
    with Anchovy Lemon Dressing & Crispy
    Breadcrumbs, 59

F

fennel (bulb)

Chicken Noodle Roast Chicken, 155–56

Vegetable Broth, 245

fish and seafood. *See also* anchovies; salmon

Baked Fish Butty, 114–15

Creamy Lobster Gnocchi, 107–8

Crispy Coconut Fish Tacos, 119–20

Lemony Piccata, 129

Lemony Shrimp with White Beans & Garlic
    Toast, 125

Pantry Puttanesca, 97

Sesame Shrimpies, 116–17

Smoked Fish Brandade, 121–22

Tomato Trout, 130

Flatbread, No-Yeast, 247

Freeze & Fry Breakfast Sausage, 16

French Onion Pot Roast with Gruyère Potatoes,
    177–78

fruit. *See also* berries; fruit, dried; *specific fruits*

Almond Cherry Brownie Pudding, 240

Balsamic Grilled Radicchio & Pears, 73

Black Forest Tart, 225–26

Cinnamon Cream Cheese & Peach Galette,
    221

Crispy Coconut Fish Tacos, 119–20

Grilled Stone-Fruit Melba, 239

Mango Salad, 138

Pizza Today/Pizza Tomorrow, 165–66

Soft Fruit Freezer Compote, 28

fruit, dried

Curried Lentil Stuffed Squash, 82

Whatever You Like Slice & Bake Cookies,
    195–96

G

garlic, 8. *See also* vegetables

Creamy Polenta with Greens, Tomatoes &
    Cheese, 88

Crispy Garlic Parmesan Potatoes with Roasted
    Garlic Mayo, 51

French Onion Pot Roast with Gruyère Potatoes,
    177–78

Fresh & Grilled Ratatouille with Provençal
    Chicken, 153–54

Hummus, 23

Lemony Shrimp with White Beans & Garlic
  Toast, 125
Mushroom Stroganoff, 91
My Go-To Pesto, 246
Roasted Garlic Bread Chicken Thighs, 149
Roasted Sausage Sheet Pan Dinner, 171
Sheet Pan Sunday Roast, 159–60
Smoked Fish Brandade, 121–22
ginger
  Creamy Harissa Lamb Meatballs, 167–68
  Ginger Molasses Cookies, 191
  Green Ginger Miso Soup, 42
  Quick Coconut Butter Tofu with Chickpeas,
    87
  Satay Chicken Wings with Peanut Sauce,
    137–38
  Seared Carrot Ginger Salmon, 126
  Sesame Shrimpies, 116–17
Gnocchi, Creamy Lobster, 107–8
grapes: Pizza Today/Pizza Tomorrow, 165–66
Green Eggs sans Ham, 20
greens, 8. See also spinach
  Balsamic Grilled Radicchio & Pears, 73
  BLT Chicken, 150
  Chipotle Chicken Soup, 139
  Creamy Polenta with Greens, Tomatoes &
    Cheese, 88
  Fried Feta Salad with Honey & Herbs, 56
  Green Couscous Salad, 55
  Green Ginger Miso Soup, 42
  Green Veg Gratin, 78
  Lemony Lentil Soup, 45
  Lemony Shrimp with White Beans & Garlic
    Toast, 125
  My Go-To Pesto, 246
  Pan-Fried Halloumi with Greens & Romesco,
    81
  Quick Coconut Butter Tofu with Chickpeas,
    87
  Romaine & Endive Salad with Anchovy
    Lemon Dressing & Crispy Breadcrumbs,
    59

Seared Carrot Ginger Salmon, 126
Spicy Sausage Pasta with Rapini & Herbed
  Ricotta, 109–10
Stewed White Beans with Greens & Chili, 84

H
Halloumi with Greens & Romesco, Pan-Fried, 81
harissa paste
  Creamy Harissa Lamb Meatballs, 167–68
  Smoky Harissa Eggplant with Herby Feta Oil
    & Pine Nuts, 74
herbs, 8. See also basil; cilantro
  Caramelized Shallots with Sherry Vinegar
    & Pistachios, 69
  Creamy Polenta with Greens, Tomatoes
    & Cheese, 88
  Fried Feta Salad with Honey & Herbs, 56
  Green Couscous Salad, 55
  Herbed Blinis a.k.a. Savory Pancakes, 15
  Roasted Mushrooms with Blue Cheese
    Rosemary Crumb, 77
  Smoky Harissa Eggplant with Herby Feta Oil
    & Pine Nuts, 74
  Spicy Sausage Pasta with Rapini & Herbed
    Ricotta, 109–10
  Tzatziki, 144
honey
  Fried Feta Salad with Honey & Herbs, 56
  Grilled Stone-Fruit Melba, 239
hot sauce
  Buffalo Roasted Cauliflower & Chickpea Pitas
    with Blue Cheese Slaw, 46–47
  Satay Chicken Wings with Peanut Sauce,
    137–38
Hummus Tartines, Red Pepper, 23

I
Irish Onion Soup, 41

J
jams & jellies (as ingredient)
  Black Forest Tart, 225–26

Creamy Polenta with Greens, Tomatoes & Cheese, 88

K

kale
Lemony Shrimp with White Beans & Garlic Toast, 125
Spicy Sausage Pasta with Rapini & Herbed Ricotta (variation), 109–10
kitchen equipment, 9

L

lamb, 7–8
Creamy Harissa Lamb Meatballs, 167–68
leeks
Chicken Noodle Roast Chicken, 155–56
Vegetable Broth, 245
lemon
Creamy Spaghetti al Limone, 94
Hummus, 23
Lemon Almond Blueberry Muffins, 24
Lemon Cornmeal Olive Oil Cake, 205–6
Lemony Lentil Soup, 45
Lemony Piccata, 129
Lemony Shrimp with White Beans & Garlic Toast, 125
Mary's Lemon Meringue Pie, 223–24
Pan-Fried Halloumi with Greens & Romesco, 81
Soft Fruit Freezer Compote, 28
Spicy Roasted Sweet Potatoes, 52
Whatever You Like Slice & Bake Cookies, 195–96
lentils
Curried Lentil Stuffed Squash, 82
Lemony Lentil Soup, 45
lettuce. See greens
lime
Crispy Coconut Fish Tacos, 119–20
Green Ginger Miso Soup, 42
Mango Salad, 138
Satay Chicken Wings with Peanut Sauce, 137–38

Spicy Roasted Sweet Potatoes, 52

M

Mango Salad, 138
maple syrup
Bistro Salad, 61–62
Curried Lentil Stuffed Squash, 82
Freeze & Fry Breakfast Sausage, 16
Marble Zucchini Loaf with Chocolate Cinnamon Streusel, 200–201
Mary's Lemon Meringue Pie, 223–24
Mediterranean Salmon, 133
milk. See also buttermilk; cream
Chocolate Hazelnut Croissant French Toast Bake, 27
Creamed Corn Baked Feta, 66
Mushroom & Pesto Skillet Lasagna, 103–4
miso paste
Green Ginger Miso Soup, 42
Miso Butter Corn Pasta, 101–2
mushrooms
Black Bean Chipotle Veggie Burger, 48–49
Green Ginger Miso Soup, 42
Mushroom & Pesto Skillet Lasagna, 103–4
Mushroom Stroganoff, 91
Roast Beef Bourguignon, 185–86
Roasted Mushrooms with Blue Cheese Rosemary Crumb, 77
My Dream Chocolate Chip Cookie, 190
My Go-To Pesto, 246

N

noodles. See also pasta
Green Ginger Miso Soup, 42
Mushroom Stroganoff, 91
No-Yeast Flatbread, 247
nuts. See also specific types of nuts
Mango Salad, 138
Quick Coconut Butter Tofu with Chickpeas, 87
Whatever You Like Slice & Bake Cookies, 195–96

O

Oat Crepes with Sweet Mascarpone & Blackberries, 33–34
oils, 7
olives
    Pantry Puttanesca, 97
    Sheet Pan Souvlaki, 143–44
onions. *See also* vegetables
    French Onion Pot Roast with Gruyère Potatoes, 177–78
    Irish Onion Soup, 41
    Roast Beef Bourguignon, 185–86
    Roasted Sausage Sheet Pan Dinner, 171
    Sheet Pan Sunday Roast, 159–60
orange
    Blackberry Apple Cream Cheese Cobbler, 228
    Cannoli Bougatsa, 231
    Oat Crepes with Sweet Mascarpone & Blackberries, 33–34
    Soft Fruit Freezer Compote, 28

P

pancetta. *See* bacon
pantry ingredients, 7–9
pasta. *See also* noodles
    Caprese Baked Rigatoni alla Vodka, 98
    Chicken Noodle Roast Chicken, 155–56
    Creamy Lobster Gnocchi, 107–8
    Creamy Spaghetti al Limone, 94
    Green Couscous Salad, 55
    Miso Butter Corn Pasta, 101–2
    Mushroom & Pesto Skillet Lasagna, 103–4
    Pantry Puttanesca, 97
    Spicy Sausage Pasta with Rapini & Herbed Ricotta, 109–10
pastry
    Basic Pastry, 213–17
    Cannoli Bougatsa, 231
    Cinnamon Cream Cheese & Peach Galette, 221
    Fresh Strawberry Pie with Stable Whipped Cream, 219
    Mary's Lemon Meringue Pie, 223–24

Pavlova, Dulce de Leche, 233–34
peaches: Cinnamon Cream Cheese & Peach Galette, 221
peanut butter
    Chocolate Peanut Butter Cake with Cornflake Crunch, 211–12
    Satay Chicken Wings with Peanut Sauce, 137–38
pears: Balsamic Grilled Radicchio & Pears, 73
pecans
    Apple Cinnamon Biscuit Buns, 31–32
    Dulce de Leche Pavlova, 233–34
    Whatever You Like Slice & Bake Cookies, 195–96
peppers, bell
    Fresh & Grilled Ratatouille with Provençal Chicken, 153–54
    Mango Salad, 138
    Pan-Fried Halloumi with Greens & Romesco, 81
    Pantry Puttanesca, 97
    Red Pepper Hummus Tartines, 23
    Roasted Sausage Sheet Pan Dinner, 171
peppers, chili
    Black Bean Chipotle Veggie Burger, 48–49
    Chipotle Breakfast Burritos, 12
    Chipotle Chicken Soup, 139
    Crispy Coconut Fish Tacos, 119–20
    Green Ginger Miso Soup, 42
    Quick Coconut Butter Tofu with Chickpeas, 87
    Satay Chicken Wings with Peanut Sauce, 137–38
    Spicy Roasted Sweet Potatoes, 52
    Stewed White Beans with Greens & Chili, 84
pesto
    Balsamic Grilled Radicchio & Pears, 73
    Caprese Baked Rigatoni alla Vodka, 98
    Green Eggs sans Ham, 20
    Mushroom & Pesto Skillet Lasagna, 103–4
    My Go-To Pesto, 246
pies and tarts
    Black Forest Tart, 225–26
    Cinnamon Cream Cheese & Peach Galette, 221

Fresh Strawberry Pie with Stable Whipped
    Cream, 219
Mary's Lemon Meringue Pie, 223–24
pineapple: Crispy Coconut Fish Tacos, 119–20
pine nuts
    BLT Chicken, 150
    Creamy Harissa Lamb Meatballs, 167–68
    My Go-To Pesto, 246
    Smoky Harissa Eggplant with Herby Feta Oil
        & Pine Nuts, 74
pistachios
    Balsamic Grilled Radicchio & Pears, 73
    Cannoli Bougatsa, 231
    Caramelized Shallots with Sherry Vinegar &
        Pistachios, 69
Pizza Today/Pizza Tomorrow, 165–66
polenta. *See* cornmeal and polenta
pork, 7–8
    Brine & Bake Pork Chops, 172
    Cider Pork Tenderloin with Autumn Veg, 175
    Creamy Harissa Lamb Meatballs (variation),
        167–68
    Freeze & Fry Breakfast Sausage, 16
potatoes
    Bistro Salad, 61–62
    Cider Pork Tenderloin with Autumn Veg
        (variation), 175
    Crispy Garlic Parmesan Potatoes with
        Roasted Garlic Mayo, 51
    Crispy Mini Rösti, 19
    French Onion Pot Roast with Gruyère Potatoes,
        177–78
    Sheet Pan Souvlaki, 143–44
    Sheet Pan Sunday Roast, 159–60
    Smoked Fish Brandade, 121–22
poultry, 7–8. *See also* chicken and turkey

Q
Quick Coconut Butter Tofu with Chickpeas, 87

R
radicchio: Balsamic Grilled Radicchio & Pears, 73

raspberries
    Grilled Stone-Fruit Melba, 239
    Raspberry Cheesecake Blondies, 197–98
rice
    Black Bean Chipotle Veggie Burger, 48–49
    Creamy Harissa Lamb Meatballs, 167–68
Romaine & Endive Salad with Anchovy Lemon
    Dressing & Crispy Breadcrumbs, 59

S
salads
    Bistro Salad, 61–62
    Fried Feta Salad with Honey & Herbs, 56
    Green Couscous Salad, 55
    Mango Salad, 138
    Romaine & Endive Salad with Anchovy
        Lemon Dressing & Crispy Breadcrumbs,
        59
    Seared Carrot Ginger Salmon, 126
salmon
    Herbed Blinis a.k.a. Savory Pancakes, 15
    Mediterranean Salmon, 133
    Seared Carrot Ginger Salmon, 126
    Smoked Fish Brandade, 121–22
salt, 7
sandwiches and burgers
    Baked Fish Butty, 114–15
    Black Bean Chipotle Veggie Burger, 48–49
    Buffalo Roasted Cauliflower & Chickpea Pitas
        with Blue Cheese Slaw, 46–47
    Red Pepper Hummus Tartines, 23
    Sesame Shrimpies, 116–17
Satay Chicken Wings with Peanut Sauce, 137–38
sausage
    Freeze & Fry Breakfast Sausage, 16
    Pizza Today/Pizza Tomorrow, 165–66
    Roasted Sausage Sheet Pan Dinner, 171
    Spicy Sausage Pasta with Rapini & Herbed
        Ricotta, 109–10
sesame oil (toasted)
    Green Ginger Miso Soup, 42
    Sesame Shrimpies, 116–17

shallots. *See also* vegetables
    Caramelized Shallots with Sherry Vinegar
      & Pistachios, 69
    Lemony Shrimp with White Beans & Garlic
      Toast, 125
    Miso Butter Corn Pasta, 101–2
    Roasted Garlic Bread Chicken Thighs, 149
sheet pan meals
    Roasted Sausage Sheet Pan Dinner, 171
    Sheet Pan Souvlaki, 143–44
    Sheet Pan Sunday Roast, 159–60
shrimp
    Lemony Shrimp with White Beans & Garlic
      Toast, 125
    Sesame Shrimpies, 116–17
soups
    Chipotle Chicken Soup, 139
    Green Ginger Miso Soup, 42
    Irish Onion Soup, 41
    Lemony Lentil Soup, 45
sour cream
    Chipotle Chicken Soup, 139
    Coconut Loaf with Chocolate Hazelnut
      Glaze, 203
    Crispy Coconut Fish Tacos, 119–20
    Crispy Mini Rösti, 19
    Herbed Blinis a.k.a. Savory Pancakes, 15
    Lemon Almond Blueberry Muffins, 24
    Lemony Lentil Soup, 45
    Mushroom Stroganoff, 91
    Spicy Roasted Sweet Potatoes, 52
    Tiramisu Cupcakes, 207–8
spices, 7
Spicy Roasted Sweet Potatoes, 52
Spicy Sausage Pasta with Rapini & Herbed
    Ricotta, 109–10
spinach. *See also* greens
    Chipotle Breakfast Burritos, 12
    Curried Lentil Stuffed Squash, 82
    Green Eggs sans Ham, 20
    Mushroom & Pesto Skillet Lasagna,
      103–4

    Spicy Sausage Pasta with Rapini & Herbed
      Ricotta (variation), 109–10
squash. *See also* zucchini
    Cider Pork Tenderloin with Autumn Veg, 175
    Curried Lentil Stuffed Squash, 82
Steak with Chimichurri, Reverse-Sear, 183
strawberries: Fresh Strawberry Pie with Stable
    Whipped Cream, 219
sweet potatoes
    Cider Pork Tenderloin with Autumn Veg
      (variation), 175
    Crispy Mini Rösti, 19
    Roasted Sausage Sheet Pan Dinner, 171
    Spicy Roasted Sweet Potatoes, 52

T

tahini
    Anchovy Lemon Dressing (variation), 59
    Hummus, 23
    Parmesan Zucchini with Crispy Chickpeas
      & Tahini Ricotta, 70
Tiramisu Cupcakes, 207–8
tofu
    Green Ginger Miso Soup, 42
    Quick Coconut Butter Tofu with Chickpeas,
      87
tomatoes. *See also* tomatoes, sun-dried;
    vegetables
    Caprese Baked Rigatoni alla Vodka, 98
    Chick Parm Meatballs, 145–46
    Chipotle Chicken Soup, 139
    Creamy Polenta with Greens, Tomatoes &
      Cheese, 88
    Eggplant Parmesan, 63–64
    Mediterranean Salmon, 133
    Pan con Tomate, 38
    Seared Carrot Ginger Salmon, 126
    Spicy Sausage Pasta with Rapini & Herbed
      Ricotta, 109–10
    Tomato Trout, 130
tomatoes, sun-dried
    BLT Chicken, 150

Pan-Fried Halloumi with Greens & Romesco, 81

Pantry Puttanesca, 97

Parmesan Zucchini with Crispy Chickpeas
    & Tahini Ricotta, 70

Sheet Pan Souvlaki, 143–44

tortillas

    Chipotle Breakfast Burritos, 12

    Crispy Coconut Fish Tacos, 119–20

tuna: Pantry Puttanesca, 97

turkey: Creamy Harissa Lamb Meatballs
    (variation), 167–68

Tzatziki, 144

V

vegetables (mixed). *See also* greens; *specific
    vegetables*

    Buffalo Roasted Cauliflower & Chickpea Pitas
        with Blue Cheese Slaw, 46–47

    Chicken Noodle Roast Chicken, 155–56

    Chicken Stock, 244

    Curried Lentil Stuffed Squash, 82

    Fresh & Grilled Ratatouille with Provençal
        Chicken, 153–54

    Vegetable Broth, 245

W

walnuts

    Black Bean Chipotle Veggie Burger, 48–49

    Creamy Harissa Lamb Meatballs, 167–68

    Curried Lentil Stuffed Squash, 82

Pizza Today/Pizza Tomorrow, 165–66

Whatever You Like Slice & Bake Cookies, 195–96

wine

    Cider Pork Tenderloin with Autumn Veg, 175

    Creamy Harissa Lamb Meatballs, 167–68

    Creamy Lobster Gnocchi, 107–8

    Fresh & Grilled Ratatouille with Provençal
        Chicken, 153–54

    Lemony Shrimp with White Beans & Garlic
        Toast, 125

    Mediterranean Salmon, 133

    Mushroom & Pesto Skillet Lasagna, 103–4

    Roast Beef Bourguignon, 185–86

Y

yogurt. *See also* sour cream

    Creamy Harissa Lamb Meatballs, 167–68

    Grilled Stone-Fruit Melba, 239

    Lemon Cornmeal Olive Oil Cake, 205–6

    Tzatziki, 144

Z

zucchini

    Fresh & Grilled Ratatouille with Provençal
        Chicken, 153–54

    Lemony Lentil Soup, 45

    Marble Zucchini Loaf with Chocolate
        Cinnamon Streusel, 200–201

    Parmesan Zucchini with Crispy Chickpeas
        & Tahini Ricotta, 70